SECURITIZATION

The Analysis
and Development of the
▶Loan-Based/Asset-Backed◀
Securities Markets

CHRISTINE A. PAVEL

Probus Publishing
Chicago, Illinois

The views expressed are those of the author and do not necessarily represent the views of the Federal Reserve Bank of Chicago or the Federal Reserve System.

This publication is designed to provide accurate and authoritative information in regard to the subject matter covered. It is sold with the understanding that the publisher is not engaged in rendering legal, accounting or other professional service. If legal advice or other expert assistance is required, the services of a competent professional person should be sought.

FROM A DECLARATION OF PRINCIPLES JOINTLY ADOPTED BY A COMMITTEE OF THE AMERICAN BAR ASSOCIATION AND A COMMITTEE OF PUBLISHERS.

Library of Congress Cataloging-in-Publication Data

Pavel, Christine.
    Securitization: the analysis and development of the loan-based/asset backed securities markets.

    Includes index.
    1. Asset-backed financing. I. Title.
HG4028.A84P38 1989   332.63'2   88-31710
ISBN 1-55738-037-6

Printed in the United States of America

1 2 3 4 5 6 7 8 9 0

bv

Dedication

To Joseph

Contents

v

Preface

Securitization, the pooling and repackaging of loans into securities, is a process that began nearly twenty years ago with residential mortgage loans and has since spread to well over a dozen types of assets. As this practice becomes even more widespread, its impact on the financial services industry as well as the success of individual issues will likely depend on a clear understanding of the costs and benefits of asset securitization by all parties involved.

This book is designed to provide such an understanding. It consists of ten chapters divided into four parts. The first explains the fundamentals of securitization—the history, basic structures, key players, and necessary components. The chapters in Part II explain the securitization of particular types of assets—mortgage loans, auto loan, credit card receivables—in greater detail. Emphasis is given to the characteristics of the assets and their primary markets as they relate to securitization as well as the characteristics of the asset-backed securities created and their risks and returns. Part III discusses the accounting, legal and regulatory environment for securitization. Part IV provides some insight into the future of securitization, how trends and developments in the economy and in the financial services industry will affect asset securitization, and how securitization will affect them.

The author wishes to thank Herbert L. Baer, Jerry Edwards, Clark M. Johnson, George G. Kaufman, Larry R. Mote, Richard Pfordte, Diana Raedle, and Donald Wilson for their invaluable comments, suggestions and insights. I would also like to thank Maureen O'Neil and the research librarians at the Federal Reserve Bank of Chicago for their excellent research assistance and the people at Probus Publishing. Without their help this project could not have been completed.

PART I
▶ Introduction ◀

CHAPTER 1

▶ Securitization Basics ◀

THE SELLING OF WHOLE LOANS and participations dates back to before the 1880s, but securitization is a recent innovation in asset sales. It involves the pooling and repackaging of loans into securities that are then sold to investors. Like whole loan sales and participations, securitization provides an additional funding source and may eliminate assets from a loan originator's balance sheet. Unlike whole loan sales and participations, securitization is often used to market small loans that would be difficult to sell on a stand-alone basis.

While the rapid growth of securitization is largely a product of the 1980s, the origin of securitization is usually traced to 1970, when the Government National Mortgage Association ("Ginnie Mae," or GNMA) developed the GNMA pass-through, a mortgage-backed security collateralized by single-family Federal Housing Administration (FHA) and Veterans Administration (VA) mortgage loans. Since then commercial banks, savings and loan associations, and various non-deposit-based firms have securitized multifamily and commercial mortgage loans, automobile loans, credit card receivables, computer and truck leases, loans for mobile homes, various trade receivables, and other types of assets. The majority of

3

asset-backed securities, nevertheless, are collateralized by single-family, residential mortgage loans.

The purpose of this chapter is to provide the reader with a basic understanding of asset securitization. The first section describes the basic structures of asset-backed securities, and the second section provides an overview of nonmortgage asset securitization. The third section discusses the costs and benefits from securitization. The fourth section looks at the factors that determine whether an asset can be securitized and examines the possibilities for further securitization.

Basic Structures

There are three basic types of asset-backed securities—pass-throughs, asset-backed bonds, and pay-throughs (see Figure 1-1). Each of these developed out of the secondary mortgage market and each has been applied to securitizing non-mortgage-related assets.

Pass-Throughs

The first type of asset-backed security was the pass-through. A pass-through represents direct ownership in a portfolio of assets that are usually similar in terms to maturity, interest rate, and quality. The portfolio is placed in trust, and certificates of ownership are sold to investors. The originator services the portfolio and collects interest and principal, passing them on, less a servicing fee, to the investors. Ownership of the assets in the portfolio lies with the investors; thus, pass-throughs are not debt obligations of the originator and do not appear on the originator's financial statement.

The most common type of pass-through is the GNMA. A GNMA pass-through is a mortgage-backed security collateralized by FHA/VA mortgage loans. The GNMA, a direct agency of the federal government, guarantees the timely payment of principal and interest. An active and well-developed secondary market provides a high degree of marketability for these secur-

Figure 1-1 Turning Loans into Securities

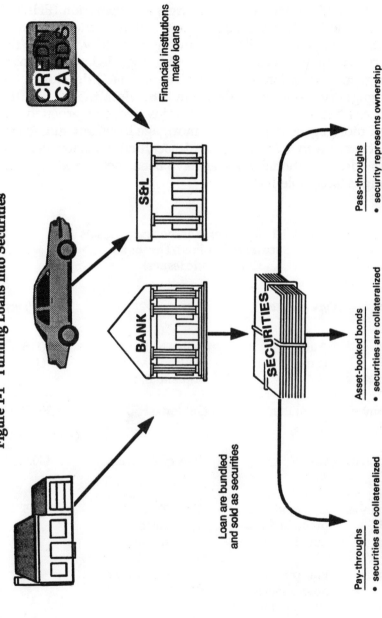

Financial institutions make loans

Loan are bundled and sold as securities

Pay-throughs
- securities are collateralized debt obligations of issues
- assets remain an originator's balance sheet
- payments of principal and interest passed through to investors

Asset-booked bonds
- securities are collateralized debt obligations of issues
- assets remain an originator's balance sheet
- payments of principal and interest passed through to investors

Pass-throughs
- security represents ownership in asset pool
- assets removed from originator's balance sheet
- payments of principal and interest passed through to investors

ities. The Federal Home Loan Mortgage Corporation (FHLMC or "Freddie Mac"), an indirect agency of the federal government, developed a similar pass-through security in 1971, the "participation certificate" (PC), and the Federal National Mortgage Association (FNMA, or "Fannie Mae") developed the mortgage-backed security (MBS) in 1981. Both the PC and the MBS are backed by portfolios of uninsured and privately insured mortgage loans. Not only mortgage loans but auto loans, credit card receivables, computer leases, and loans for pleasure boats and recreational vehicles have been securitized as pass-throughs (see Table 1-1).

Table 1-1   Types of Nonmortgage Assets
Securitized as Pass-Throughs
(First Public Issues)

Date	Type of Asset	Issuer	$Millions
May 1985	Auto loans	Valley National Bank and Marine Midland Banks	100.5 60.2
December 1986	Computer leases	Goldome FSB	205.7
February 1987	Credit cards	Bank of America	400.0
September 1987	Conventional manufactured home loans	Green Tree Acceptance Corporation	71.5
October 1987	Equipment notes financing leveraged leases	American Airlines	92.6

Source: *Asset Sales Report*, various issues.

Asset-Backed Bonds

The second type of asset-backed security, the asset-backed bond (ABB), is patterned after the mortgage-backed bond (MBB). Like the pass-through, the ABB is collateralized by a portfolio of loans or sometimes by a portfolio of pass-through securities such as GNMAs. Unlike the pass-through, the ABB is a debt obligation of the issuer, so the portfolio of loans used as collateral remains on the issuer's books as assets and the ABBs are reported as liabilities. Also, the cash flows from the collateral are not dedicated to the payment of principal and interest on ABBs.

One important characteristic of ABBs is that they are usually overcollateralized. The collateral is evaluated quarterly, and if its value falls below the level stated in the bond indenture, more loans or securities must be added to the collateral.

There are three reasons for the overcollateralization of ABBs. First, because the cash flows accrue to the issuer rather than to the loan pool or to the bondholders, the outstanding balance of any pool of loans may decline faster over time than the principal on the ABBs. Second, the excess collateral provides additional protection to the bondholder against default on individual loans in the pool. Third, the excess collateral protects bondholders from declines in the market value of the collateral between valuation dates. Premiums for the risk of default and collateral depreciation could be captured in the yield on ABBs; however, because payment of principal and interest accrues to the issuer and can be used for reinvestment the issuer may prefer to use overcollaterization.

Many types of nonmortgage-related assets have been securitized as ABBs. As shown in Table 1-2, computer and automobile leases, auto loans, and junk bonds have collateralized note issues sold publicly. Loans for employee stock ownership plans and premium loans have been securitized as notes through private placements.

**Table 1-2 Types of Nonmortgage Assets
Securitized as Asset-Backed Bonds and Pay-Throughs
(First Public Issues)**

Date	Type of Asset	Issuer	$Millions	Structure
March 1985	Computer leases	Sperry	$192.5	Pay-throughs
July 1986	Auto loans	Chrysler	205.7	Pay-throughs
October 1986	Auto loans	GMAC	4,000.0	ABBs
January 1987	Credit cards	RepublicBank	199.5	Pay-throughs
September 1987	Junk bonds	Imperial Savings	100.0	ABBs
October 1987	Auto leases	Volkswagen	150.0	ABBs
November 1987	Consumer loans	Household FSB	432.1	Pay-throughs

Source: *Asset Sales Report,* various issues.

Pay-Throughs

The third type of asset-backed security is the pay-through bond. This bond combines some of the features of the pass-through with some of those of the asset-backed bond. The bond is collateralized by a pool of assets and appears on the is-suer's financial statements as debt. The cash flows from the as-sets, however, are dedicated to servicing the bonds in a way similar to that of pass-throughs.

In June 1983, Freddie Mac issued a pay-through bond known as the CMO (collateralized mortgage obligation). This type of pay-through directs the cash flows in order to support bonds of various maturities, rather than bonds with maturities that only match that of the underlying portfolio. Freddie Mac's original CMO issue was divided into three maturity classes, and each class received semiannual interest payments. Since Freddie Mac developed the first CMO, many variations have been developed. Issues of CMOs now have from three to more than six maturity classes. Most CMO issues, however, have four maturity classes.

The pay-through structure has been applied to non-mortgage-related assets, such as auto loans, credit card receivables, and unsecured consumer loans. Through private placements, the pay-through structure has also been used to securitize life insurance policyholder loans.

Asset-Backed Commercial Paper and Preferred Stock

In addition to collateralized bonds and pay-through notes, commercial paper and preferred stock have also been backed by certain assets. Credit card receivables, automobile and utility leases, and trade receivables have served as collateral for commercial paper. Preferred stock has been backed by mortgage-backed securities and trade receivables.

Like asset-backed bonds, asset-backed commercial paper and preferred stock are usually issued through finance companies organized for the sole purpose of issuing the asset-backed securities and buying the underlying assets with the proceeds. Also like asset-backed bonds, asset-backed commercial paper is usually credit enhanced with an irrevocable letter of credit and with overcollateralization. Commercial paper is often backed with a line of credit from a commercial bank to make up for any deficiencies in the cash flows of the underlying assets due to losses, delinquencies, or mismatch of payments.

Unlike asset-backed bonds, asset-backed commercial paper and preferred stock do not have interest or dividend payments tied to the cash flows of the underlying assets. Asset-backed preferred stock is auction-rated; that is, the dividends are reset every periodically in an auction process, which keeps the price of the stock at par, while allowing the yield to reflect current market rates adjusted to account for the favorable tax treatment afforded corporate investors of preferred stock.

Nonmortgage Asset-Backed Securities

The bulk of nonmortgage-related assets securitized so far consists mostly of auto loans and credit card receivables. As shown in Table 1-3, however, over 10 types of assets other than residential mortgage loans were securitized during 1987.

Table 1-3   The Market for Securitization: 1987
($Millions)

	Total Securitized*
Residential mortgages	$323,000.0
Multifamily mortgages	5,796.00
Auto loans	6,368.8
Credit card receivables	2,409.5
Leases receivables	150.0
Other consumer loans	432.1
Trade receivables	311.5
Manufactured home loans	
FHA/VA	815.6
Conventional	439.5**
Junk bonds	100.0

* Publicly issued only unless otherwise noted.
**Includes some private placements.

Sources: *Asset Sales Report*, various issues; Federal Home Loan Mortgage Corporation; and Government National Mortgage Association.

Automobile loans were first packaged and sold as securities in 1985, when Salomon Brothers offered $60 million of pass-through securities backed by automobile loans originated and serviced by Marine Midland Bank. These and other auto loan-backed securities were dubbed certificates of automobile receivables—CARs. They are pass-through securities in which the interest and principal of the underlying auto loans are passed on to the security holders. Since 1985, over $15 billion of automobile loans have been securitized in public offerings. Chapter 4 discusses securities backed by automobile loans in more detail.

Based on dollar volume, credit card receivables have been the third most securitized asset. In April 1986, Salomon Brothers privately placed $50 million of pass-throughs backed by a pool of Bank One credit card receivables known as "certificates of amortizing revolving debts" (CARDs). By June 1988, nine public issues of securities backed by credit card receivables had come to market, representing nearly two percent of all credit card receivables outstanding. A more detailed discussion of securities backed by credit card debt can be found in Chapter 5.

Other types of securitized loans include loans guaranteed by the Small Business Administration, computer leases, various types of trade credit, and other consumer loans, such as mobile home, recreational vehicle, and boat loans. While most consumer loans have been securitized as pass-through securities, securities involving lease receivables and trade credit have been structured as asset-backed bonds. The securitization of lease receivables, SBA loans, consumer loans other than auto and credit card debt, and other types of assets including commercial loans is discussed in more detail in Chapter 6.

Why Securitize?

A pool of loans will, of course, be securitized only if the benefits from doing so exceed the costs, and if the net benefits are greater than those from holding the assets on the balance sheet (see Figure 1-2). The primary costs of securitization are the administrative costs, such as the investment banking fee, the fee to the rating agencies, the fee for filing with the Securities and Exchange Commission and the National Association of Securities Dealers, the fee to the trustee, and in some instances, the cost of private insurance. As shown in Table 1-4, the cost can typically amount to 60 to 100 basis points, depending on the level of credit enhancement and the size of the offering.

Figure 1-2   Cost versus Benefits from Securitization

Source: Federal Reserve Bank of Chicago.

Table 1-4   Costs of Securitization
($100 Million Public Auto Loan Issue)

Gross proceeds from offering	$100,000
Less: Underwriting fee	300-500
Proceeds to issuer	99,700-99,500
= Less: Issuance expenses	
Credit enhancement	50-140
SEC, NASD, Blue Sky filing	80
Rating agency fee	30-60
Printing and engraving	20-40
Accounting	20-50
Trustee's fee	40-50
Legal	60-100
	300-520
Proceeds net of issuance expense	99,400-98,980
As a percentage of gross offering	99.4-98.98

Source: Salomon Brothers and Security Pacific Auto Finance.

The benefits from securitization include protection from interest-rate risk (and sometimes prepayment risk), increased liquidity and diversification for original lenders and for investors, a more efficient flow of capital from investors to borrowers, and creation of a new and less expensive funding source for original lenders. Securitization may enable institutions to attract long-term funds more profitably than would be possible with conventional tools, and it can also provide the originator with a new source of fee income from originating and servicing the securitized assets.

Securitization can increase the liquidity of a loan portfolio by making it possible to package and sell these otherwise illiquid assets in an established secondary market. Greater diversification can be achieved because an institution can hold the same dollar amount of a particular type of loan in the form of a security backed by the loans of numerous borrowers, as opposed to holding whole loans of relatively few borrowers.

Protection from interest-rate risk is particularly beneficial to long-term lenders, such as savings and loan associations (S&Ls). As the primary suppliers of mortgage credit, S&Ls hold residential mortgages with average stated maturities of 27.5 years and fixed interest rates. Although originations of adjustable-rate mortgages have been increasing, 53 percent of all residential mortgage loans held by S&Ls are still fixed-rate loans.[1] More than half of the typical S&L's liabilities, primarily time and savings deposits, mature in one year or less. This gross mismatching of maturities leaves S&Ls open to the risk that interest rates will rise. Savings institutions have several techniques available to hedge interest-rate risk. For example, they can utilize the options and futures markets. These techniques, however, can be costlier than securitization, and thrift managers may be more familiar with securitization than with other gap-management tools.

Pass-through mortgage securities, as well as mortgage-backed bonds and pay-through bonds, allow S&Ls to reduce the maturity gap between their assets and liabilities. With pass-throughs, an S&L sells a pool of mortgages; thus, the long-term assets are taken off its books, shortening the average maturity of its assets and decreasing its required level of capital. The thrift, however, continues to service the loans and collects the servicing fees. Pass-throughs, therefore, have the added advantage of allowing the issuer to earn income on fewer assets and less capital, thereby greatly improving its return on assets and equity.

With mortgage-backed bonds and pay-through bonds, the portfolio of loans remains on the issuer's books, serving as collateral for the bonds. The issuer, therefore, increases its leverage by issuing more debt; however, by issuing the bonds, the issuer lengthens the average maturity of its liabilities. A mortgage-backed bond has an average maturity of about five

1 Federal Home Loan Bank Board.

to 12 years, while most deposits have maturities of less than one year.

Securitization also provides for a more efficient flow of funds from investors to borrowers. Large institutional investors, such as insurance companies and pension funds, have long-term liabilities; however, they generally do not have decentralized investment operations or distribution systems that allow them to make residential mortgages directly. Savings institutions, as already discussed, have very short-term liabilities and extensive branching networks, giving them an advantage in originating residential mortgage loans and other types of consumer loans. Securitization links the long-term funds of insurance companies and pension funds with the long-term assets of thrifts, thus allowing more capital to flow into the primary markets for credit.

Securitization may also provide a firm with a relatively inexpensive source of funds and free it from a dependency on an inelastic supply of retail deposits. For example, a bank or thrift may have to increase the rate it pays on savings deposits from 8 percent to 9 percent to attract additional funds. Alternatively, it could issue asset-backed bonds at 10 percent. The marginal cost of issuing the asset-backed bonds may be less than that of raising deposit funds because the higher rate paid on savings deposits will have to be paid on all deposits, old and new.

Securitization can provide an inexpensive funding source when a firm's overall credit rating is lower than the credit rating on its receivables. For instance, Gelco Corp., a firm that leases trucks, was rated BB—by Standard & Poor's. Its commercial paper backed by high-quality leases was rated A-1. The firm saved about 80 basis points in borrowing costs by securitizing its lease receivables.[2] Similarly, securitization can enable small and new companies to offer customer financing.

Finally, securitization can also provide a depository institution with an inexpensive source of funds because, in some

---

2 Harvey D. Shapiro, "The Securitization of Practically Everything," *Institutional Investor* 19, (May 1985), p. 201.

Finally, securitization can also provide a depository institution with an inexpensive source of funds because, in some cases, it can enable the institution to avoid "regulatory taxes," i.e., reserve and capital requirements and deposit insurance premiums. If a depository institution sells pass-through securities, it eliminates the underlying loans from its balance sheet and, therefore, no longer has to hold capital against these loans. Since the proceeds from the sale of pass-throughs are not deposits, the issuer does not have to hold reserves or pay for deposit insurance against the proceeds. These regulatory taxes have been estimated to be as low as 29 basis points and as high as 52 basis points on a riskless asset (see Figure 1-3). They would be lower for risky assets. As "regulatory taxes" increase, this benefit from securitization, and therefore securitization itself, would be expected to increase as well.

Figure 1-3   The Burden of Regulation

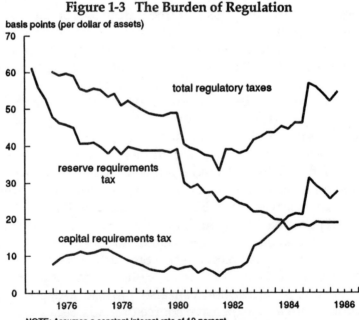

NOTE: Assumes a constant interest rate of 10 percent.

Source: Herbert L. Baer and Christine A. Pavel, "Does Regulation Drive Innovation?" *Economic Perspectives*, Federal Reserve Bank of Chicago, March/April 1988.

To the extent that regulatory taxes are too high on some types of bank assets, securitization may be a reaction to these taxes. For example, deposit insurance and capital requirements are flat taxes; thus, high-risk loans are taxed at the same rate as low-risk loans. The "after-tax" cost of funding low-risk loans may be higher than the costs faced by nonregulated competitors or by the borrowers themselves.

Can Everything Be Securitized?

Not all assets are easy to securitize. Loan terms, borrower characteristics, and structures vary significantly. Also, the benefits to any individual firm from securitization depend upon each firm's particular situation and upon the type of asset securitized. The costs of securitizing are not the same for different types of assets.

The riskiness of an asset-backed security is the main determinant of its price. The riskier the security, the lower the price, and therefore the higher the yield. If the yield on the security is greater than the average yield on the underlying pool of loans, the benefits from securitizing may be eliminated. In addition, if securities are rated below investment grade by the credit rating agencies, then regulated financial institutions usually will not invest in them because they have to justify such investments to their regulators.

Several options to decrease the riskiness of an issue are available to a securities issuer, however. For asset-backed bonds a high degree of overcollateralization will increase the safety of the bonds and decrease the required return. Another way to increase the safety of an issue is to insure the securities themselves.

When an issuer of asset-backed securities uses a private firm to insure the loans or the portfolio underlying the securities, the issuer passes the default risk on to the insurer. The premium that the insurer charges is compensation for the default risk and the cost of evaluating the portfolio. The cost of evaluating complicated portfolios may eliminate the benefits of securitization. Therefore, the easier a portfolio is to evaluate, the more likely that it will be securitized.

The ability to evaluate the pool of loans that underlies a security issue, and therefore the securities themselves, seems to be the key to securitization (see Figure 1-4). The credit characteristics of the underlying portfolio must be understandable to the credit rating agencies and to investors. Loans that are very large or that have complex credit characteristics are better suited for whole loan sales or loan participations. Other important credit characteristics for securitization include a well-defined payments pattern and a sufficiently long maturity, at least 18 months to two years.

Mortgage loans are illustrative of characteristics that make a loan a prime candidate for securitization. Residential fixed-rate mortgage loans are relatively homogeneous products and easy to evaluate. There is a secondary market for whole mortgage loans, and a wealth of data is collected on mortgage loans. Data on delinquencies, prepayments, and changes in the value of collateral broken down by various demographic characteristics are available. Also, the structures and terms of mortgage loans, at least fixed-rate mortgage loans, are similar. And because most mortgage loans are prepaid, the ex-post average maturity is about 12 years.

Figure 1-4   Ideal Asset Characteristics for Securitization

- Understandable credit characteristics
- Well-defined payments pattern/predictable cash flows
- Average maturity of at least one year
- Low delinqency and low default rates
- Total amortization
- Diverse obligors
- High liquidation value

Source: The First Boston Corporation.

Historically, mortgage loans have had excellent credit characteristics. For example, delinquency rates are quite low, although a few years ago mortgage deliquency rates had reached record levels. The delinquency rate on conventional residential mortgages was three percent of the total number of loans outstanding at year end of 1987, and had been falling since 1985.[3] The collateral backing mortgage loans contributes to their excellent credit characteristics. A single-family home is relatively easy to value and its value does not depreciate as fast as that of other forms of collateral. In fact, it often appreciates. During the 1970s, housing prices soared, so the value of collateral backing many mortgages far exceeded the balance due on the loan. Also, these mortgages were not prepaid quickly because interest rates rose during this period as well.

Besides residential mortgages, consumer loans such as auto loans, credit card receivables, lease receivables, and loans for boats and mobile homes are probably the best candidates for securitization. Each of these types of loans possesses characteristics similar to those of residential mortgage loans, and each of these types of loans has been securitized.

Commercial and industrial (C&I) loans are relatively difficult to securitize. One type of commercial loan, however, that has been securitized is that guaranteed by the Small Business Administration. The structure of these loans is fairly standard, and the federal government assumes much of the credit risk of an SBA loan by guaranteeing nearly all of the loan amount.

Nonguaranteed C&I loans are probably be the most difficult to securitize, and to date, few have been. C&I loans are not homogeneous, and the terms and structures of C&I loans vary. For example, the maturity of C&I loans ranges from less than one year to about eight years. The pricing of C&I loans also varies, and the stream of payments from a C&I loan is not fixed. C&I loans are also repriced frequently, and the timing of payments is generally tailored to meet the needs of the in-

---

3 Mortgage Bankers Association of America, *National Delinquency Survey*, February 29, 1988.

dividual borrower. Another complication in evaluating C&I loans is that their credit characteristics (e.g., default and delinquency rates and collateralization) vary greatly. These characteristics make evaluating a portfolio of C&I loans difficult.

In addition to the technical difficulties in securitizing C&I loans, there are less costly alternatives, including whole loan sales, participations, syndications, and commercial paper. At the end of June 1988, eight large commercial banks that are active sellers of whole loans and participations reported over $40 billion of loans sold or participated outstanding, which represents nearly 10 percent of their total assets and more than a 50 percent increase from a year ealier.[4]

More to Come

The following chapter discusses the primary participants and components involved in asset securitization and describes how they come together in the issuance of asset-backed securities. This process is largely dependent on the regulatory, accounting, and legal environments for asset securitization as well as on the specific characteristics of the assets being securitized. Part II discusses the securitization of specific types of assets in greater detail. The regulatory, accounting and legal aspects of securitization are discussed in Part III of the book. Finally, in Part IV, the implications of securitization for the financial services industry are discussed.

---

4 *Asset Sales Report,* various issues.

CHAPTER 2

▶ Players ◀
and Pieces

THE ISSUANCE OF ASSET-BACKED SECURITIES involves many players and pieces. This chapter discusses the players and pieces, and although all are not necessarily involved in every issue, brings most of them together in two "typical" deals—one structured as interests in a pool of assets (pass-throughs) and the other as collateralized debt (asset-backed bonds). A more detailed discussion of the various structures that are specific to the assets securitized can be found in following chapters.

The primary players involved in the issuance of asset-backed securities include the originator, servicer, issuer, investment banker, rating agencies, credit enhancer, trustee, and investors. These players establish the pieces in an asset-backed securities issue. The originator creates the underlying assets that are sold or used as collateral; the investment banker and originator establish the structure and issuing vehicle; the rating agencies, the rating; the credit enhancers, the credit enhancement; and the trustee, the trust and the certificates.

Originators

Originators create and usually service the assets that are sold or used as collateral for asset-backed securities. To date, originators have included captive finance companies of the "Big Three" auto makers, other finance companies, commercial banks, thrift institutions, computer companies, airlines, manufacturers, insurance companies, and securities firms.

Table 2-1 lists these types of firms along with the primary assets that each securitizes, which generally represent the greatest share of assets on their balance sheets. As this table shows, the auto captives, of course, securitize automobile loans, and GMAC is by far the dominant originator of assets that support securities backed by auto loans, securitizing $6.8 billion—nearly half of all securities backed by auto loans issued as of June 1988. Savings and loan associations mostly securitize residential mortgage loans either as pass-throughs, pay-throughs or mortgage-backed bonds. Savings and loans have also sold auto loans and credit card receivables. Of the loans sold by commercial banks, commercial and industrial loans represent the largest share, but commercial loans made by banks have infrequently been securitized. Banks have, however, regularly securitized auto loans, credit card receivables, and mortgage loans.

Servicers

Originators, or affiliates of originators, are usually also the servicers of the loans they sell or use as collateral. Servicers are responsible for the management and maintenance of the assets and the cash flows from those assets. That is, they are responsible for collecting principal and interest payments on the assets when due and for pursuing the collection of delinquent accounts.

Servicers are also responsible for providing the trustee and the certificate holders with monthly and annual reports concerning the portfolio of assets sold or used as collateral. The

Table 2-1 Issuers of Asset-Backed Securities

Issuer	*Primary Asset Securitized*
Federal mortgage agencies (GNMA, FNMA, and FHLMC)	Residential mortgage loans
Commercial banks	Auto loans
Savings and loans associations	Residential mortgage loans
Auto captive finance companies (GMAC, CFC, FMCC, etc.)	Auto loans and leases
Other finance companies	Auto loans, mobile home loans
Computer companies	Computer leases
Manufacturers	Trade receivables
Life insurance companies	Policyholder loans
Securities firms	Mortgage loans (CMOs)

reports detail the sources of distributed funds (principal vs. interest), the remaining principal balance, the remaining insurance amount, the amount of fees payable out of the trust, and information necessary for certificate holders to prepare their taxes. Before this information is forwarded to the certificate holders, the trustee determines whether or not the information complies with the requirements of the pooling and servicing agreement.

Issuers

Assets are not usually sold by the originator to third-party investors directly as asset-backed securities. Instead, they are sold first to a conduit or to a "bankruptcy remote" finance company. Such finance companies, known as limited purpose corporations, are separately incorporated subsidiaries or affiliates of either the originator or the underwriter. They facilitate the sale of the assets or the issuance of collateralized debt instruments. A finance company created by the underwriter is known as an "orphan subsidiary."

Issuers become bankruptcy-remote by limiting their activities to issuing asset-backed securities and using the proceeds to buy the assets that back the securities. To ensure that bankruptcy proceedings against the issuing corporation are not undertaken, no other debt is incurred or, if it is, steps are taken by the issuer to ensure that the asset-backed securities would not be affected if the corporation defaulted on other debt issues. These steps include limiting any additional debt to that which carries the same rating as the asset-backed securities and prohibiting the corporation from selling its assets unless the purchaser is bankruptcy-remote and subject to the lien of the debtholders.[1]

Conduits are issuers of asset-backed securities that do not originate or necessarily service the assets that underlie the securities. Conduits are companies that buy assets from many different originators or sellers, pool the assets, and then sell them to investors. Servicing usually remains in the hands of the originator of the assets. Conduits are particularly useful for firms that do not have enough assets to package as asset-backed securities themselves. The largest conduits are the federal mortgage agencies. They buy residential mortgage loans from savings and loans, mortgage bankers, and commercial banks, pool them into packages of loans, and then sell securities backed by the packages to investors.

Other conduits exist for Small Business Adminstration (SBA) loans, consumer loans, and commercial loans. For SBA loans, investment banks act as conduits for approved SBA lenders. While the SBA has pooled loans for many years, it was not until 1985 that it issued guidelines for pooling. These guidelines encouraged banks to standardize SBA loan contracts somewhat and consequently allowed the market for SBA loan

---

1 Standard & Poor's Corporation, *S&P's Structured Finance Criteria*, 1988.

pools to broaden. Stephens Inc., an investment bank based in Arkansas, has been positioning itself as a conduit for consumer loans, and Diversified Financial of San Francisco has recently begun trying to pool the commercial loans of banks.

When assets are not sold first to a limited purpose corporation or to a conduit, they are usually sold directly to a trust. The use of trusts is discussed later in this chapter.

Investment Bankers

An asset-backed securities issue usually involves an investment banker who either underwrites the securities for public offering or privately places them. As an underwriter, the investment bank purchases the securities from the issuer for resale. In a private placement, the investment bank does not purchase the securities and resell them; rather, the investment bank acts as an agent for the issuer, matching the seller with a handful of buyers.

For the issuer, there are tradeoffs to be made between a private placement and a public offering. Private placements are usually quicker and less expensive to issue than public offerings because private placements are exempt from registration with the Securities and Exchange Commission. To qualify for this exemption, the issuer must meet certain criteria, including no general public solicitation (except for some small issues) and limitations on the number and sophistication of purchasers. Because the investment bank assumes no underwriting risk in a private placement, the investment banking fee is generally lower for private placements than for public offerings. Private placements, however, are relatively illiquid and are limited to smaller issues because they can be sold to only a small number of investors. Therefore, while issuing costs are lower for private placements, the issuer pays an interest rate premium on privately placed debt issues.

Underwriters of publicly offered asset-backed securities as well as firms that privately place such securities have been investment banks and investment banking affiliates of commercial banks. However, because the permissibility of underwriting asset-backed securities by commercial bank-affiliated firms is unclear, as of June 1988, only a few commercial bank-affiliated firms had underwritten issues of asset-backed securities.[2]

As of December 1987, many investment banks were involved in asset-backed securities issues, but only eight investment banks were lead managers for public offerings of nonmortgage asset-backed securities. As shown in Table 2-2, the investment banking firms that dominate are First Boston and Salomon Brothers. First Boston underwrote 38 percent of the publicly offered asset-backed securities through yearend 1987, representing 50 percent of the dollar volume. Salomon Brothers was the underwriter for 22 percent of the asset-backed securities publicly offered and 28 percent of the dollar volume. First Boston was the underwriter for nearly half the securities backed by auto loans that have been publicly offered and 62 percent of the dollar volume. Salomon Brothers underwrote 43 percent of the publicly offered securities backed by credit card receivables, representing nearly one half of the dollar volume issued as of December 1987.

Although commercial banks or subsidiaries of bank holding companies have not underwritten many public offerings of asset-backed securities, they have played a significant role in privately placing asset-backed securities. As Table 2-3 shows, $23 billion of securitized assets were privately placed in 1987. This figure, which includes mortgage pass-throughs, pay-throughs, and CMOs, is about equal to the dollar amount of nonmortgage assets securitized and sold publicly in 1987. Eight commercial banks or subsidiaries of bank holding companies privately placed 136 issues (32 percent) in 1987, valued at $7.9 billion (34 percent). Three commercial banks—Bankers

---

2 The authority of commercial banking firms to underwrite asset-backed securities is discussed in detail in Chapter 9.

Trust, Citicorp, and Chase—ranked among the top 10 firms in the private placement of asset-backed securities and accounted for 22 percent of asset-backed securities privately placed in 1987.

Table 2-2 Top Underwriters of Nonmortgage Asset-Backed Securities: (Public offerings during 1987)

All nonmortgage ABSs	No. of Issues	% of Total	$ Millions	% of Total
First Boston	14	37.8%	$5,128.8	50.0%
Salomon Brothers	8	21.6	2,830.5	27.6
Goldman Sachs	4	10.8	971.6	9.5
Drexel Burnham Lambert	5	13.5	544.1	5.3
Shearson Lehman Hutton	1	2.7	215.2	2.1
Merrill Lynch	2	5.4	183.5	1.8
Dillon Read	1	2.7	150.0	1.5
Kidder Peabody	1	2.7	146.9	1.4
Morgan Stanley	1	2.7	92.6	0.9

Securities backed by auto loans:

First Boston	10	47.6%	$3,917.3	61.5%
Salomon Brothers	5	23.8	1,630.5	25.6
Drexel Burnham Lambert	4	19.0	444.1	7.0
Goldman Sachs	1	4.8	230.0	3.6
Kidder Peabody	1	4.8	146.9	2.3

Securities backed by credit card receivables:

Salomon Brothers	3	42.9%	$1,200.0	49.8%
First Boston	2	28.6	900.0	37.4
Goldman Sachs	2	28.6	309.5	12.8

Source: *Asset Sales Report,* various issues.

Table 2-3   Private Placements of Asset-Backed Securities*
During 1987
($ Millions)

	Manager	Amount	Percent	Number of Issues
1.	First Boston	$3,404	14.6%	54
2.	Goldman Sachs	2,661	11.4	18
3.	Bankers Trust	1,974	8.5	19
4.	Citicorp	1,816	7.8	49
5.	Salomon Brothers	1,753	7.5	71
6.	Shearson Lehman Hutton	1,694	7.3	36
7.	Drexel Burham Lambert	1,540	6.6	35
8.	Kidder Peabody	1,404	6.0	31
9.	Chase	1,371	5.9	30
10.	Bear Stearns	1,300	5.6	1
11.	Chemical Bank	1,036	4.4	9
12.	Morgan Graranty	803	3.4	3
13.	Morgan Stanley	609	2.6	12
14.	Merrill Lynch Capital Markets	533	2.3	8
15.	Security Pacific National Bank	475	2.0	4
16.	Bank of America	225	1.0	20
17.	Paine Webber	218	0.9	5
18.	Prudential Bache	164	0.7	4
19.	First National Bank of Chicago	157	0.7	2
20.	L.F. Rothschild	133	0.6	2
	Industry Total	$23,330		419

---

*Equal credit is assigned to each manager, includes mortgage-backed securities.

Source: *Asset Sales Report*, March 21, 1988, p. 5.

In an asset-backed security issue, whether an investment bank functions as an underwriter or privately places the securities, it is instrumental in structuring the issue. The issuer and underwriter work together to see that the structure of the issue meets all the legal, regulatory, accounting, and tax objectives. The length of time required to bring an issue to market and the degree of involvement of the investment bank in structuring the deal are greater for an issue that is the first for a particular issuer, an issue of an infrequent issuer, a new type of issue, and an issue that is a new twist on an old theme.

In addition to working closely with the issuer in structuring asset-backed securities issues, investment bankers also work with the credit enhancers, rating agencies, and trustees.

Credit Enhancers

Credit enhancement is a vehicle that reduces the overall credit risk of a security issue. The purpose of the credit enhancement is to improve the rating, and therefore the pricing and marketability, of an asset-backed security. Most asset-backed securities are credit enhanced. Credit enhancement can be provided by the issuer or by a third party; sometimes more than one type of credit enhancement supports an issue. Credit enhancement provided by a third-party has taken the form of either a letter of credit from a bank with a high credit rating or an insurance bond also from a firm with a high rating. Credit has been enhanced by the issuer by providing recourse, a senior-subordinated structure, overcollaterization, or a spread account.

In a senior-subordinated structure, two classes of asset-backed securities are issued—one senior and the other junior. The originator assumes credit risk by retaining the junior (subordinated) class of securities.

Overcollateralization in used primarily in asset-backed securities offers that are structured as debt rather than as a sale. The value of the collateral behind the debt is greater than the face value of the debt at the time of issue. If the value of the collateral falls below some predetermined dollar amount during the life of the debt, the issuer may have to add collateral. Over-collateralization protects the investor against declines in the value of the debt due to defaults and delinquencies, prepayments, and falls in the market value of the collateral.

A spread account is a fund that can be drawn upon to supplement payments to investors when the cash flows generated from the securitized assets fall short. Initially, the servicer makes an advance to the spread account. Throughout the life of the issue, the value of the spread account increases when the cash flows generated from the securitized assets exceed the funds necessary to pay investors and to pay the servicing fee. The value of the spread account falls when the cash flows from the securitized assets are insufficient to pay investors. Any funds in the spread account when the issue matures belong to the servicer.

For sale structures, letters of credit and insurance bonds are the most common types of credit enhancement. As shown in Table 2-4, from 1985 through 1987, 71 percent of asset-backed securities issued and 70 percent of the dollar volume of those issues were credit enhanced by a third-party letter of credit or insurance bond.

Table 2-4   Third-Party Credit Enhancement

Number of Issues	*1985*	*1986*	*1987*	*Total*
Total issues	7	17	38	62
Enhanced issues	6	10	28	44
Percent	86%	59%	74%	71%
Amount issued ($Millions)				
Total issues	1,227	10,000	10,763	21,763
Enhanced issues	702	5,961	8,658	15,321
Percent	57%	59%	80%	70%

Source: Union Bank of Switzerland.

As shown in Table 2-5, there are seven firms that provide credit enhancement, or third-party guarantees, for asset-backed securities in 1987. Of the seven, five are banks, four foreign and one domestic; the others include an insurer and the Federal Home Loan Bank of San Francisco. Union Bank of Switzerland has issued the most guarantees, covering the greatest dollar volume, of asset-backed securities; however, Financial Security Assurance is ultimately liable for the greatest amount. This is because Financial Security Assurance guarantees 100 percent of the principal and interest of all the securities it has guaranteed, while Union Bank of Switzerland, as well as the other credit enhancers, guarantees less than 100 percent (usually between 5 and 25 percent) of the value of any issue.

Table 2-5 Credit Enhancers for ABSs: 1987
($ Millions)

Credit Enhancer	No.of Issues	Value of Issues	Amount Guaranteed	Avg. Level of Enhancement
Union Bank of Switzerland	11	$4,640.3	498.7	10.7%
Financial Security Assurance	5	506.6	506.6	100.0
Credit Suisse	4	2,440.7	400.9	16.4
Bayerische Vereinsbank	2	402.0	38.2	9.5
Federal Home Loan Bank of San Francisco	2	210.0	37.0	17.6
Deutsche Bank	1	150.0	27.0	18.0
Morgan Guaranty	1	124.5	6.2	5.0
Other*	2	183.5	41.0	22.3

*Banks that provided only part of an issuer's guanrantee

Source: *Asset Sales Report*, February 1, 1988, p. 5.

Table 2-6   Third-Party Credit Enhancement Levels

Type of Asset Securitized	*Enhancement Level*
Auto loans	6% to 22%
Credit card receivables	5% to 35%
Lease	18% to 20%
Trucks	16%
Manufactured housing	22%

Source: Union Bank of Switzerland, Moody's Investor Service, and Standard & Poor's.

The level of credit enhancement varies by type of assets securitized and within type by the default history of the issuer's portfolio. As shown in Table 2-6, the range of credit enhancement required to achieve a AA or AAA rating has been quite large. The amount guaranteed ranges from five percent to 35 percent of the value of the underlying assets. The level required for a particular rating is largely determined by the rating agencies. Riskier deals require a higher level of credit enhancement.

Rating Agencies

Credit rating agencies assign ratings to asset-backed securities issues just as they do to corporate bonds. The credit rating is an assessment of credit risk. It is based on three criteria: the probability of the issuer's defaulting on the obligation, the nature and provisions of the obligation, and the relative position of the obligation in the event of bankruptcy.

Moody's, Standard & Poor's, Duff & Phelps, and Fitch rate asset-backed securities. The highest rating is Aaa from Moody's, AAA from Standard & Poor's and from Fitch, and D&P-1 from Duff and Phelps (see Table 2-7). All nonmortgage asset-backed securites rated by S&P to date have been initially rated AAA or AA, and all nonmortgage asset-backed securities rated by Moody's have been initially rated Aaa, Aa1, Aa2, or Aa3. Most of the issues rated by Duff & Phelps have been rated D&P-1, although one carries a rating of D&P-5. No publicly offered nonmortgage asset-backed deal has gone unrated.

In rating a corporate bond, rating agencies usually evaluate the issuer's creditworthiness. In asset-backed securities issues, however, the probability of default is not related to the issuer's creditworthiness, but rather to the credit quality of the assets that underlie the securities. Therefore, rating agencies rate asset-backed securities by assessing the ability of the underlying assets (not the issuer) to generate cash flows used for principal and interest payments to investors. In rating an asset-backed securities issue, the rating agencies analyze the structure and assess the credit enhancement.

Table 2-7 Ratings of Asset-Backed Securities

	Highest----------------------------------*Lowest*			
Duff & Phelps				
Rating	D&P-1	D&P-2,3,4	D&P-5,6,7	D&P-8,9,10
No. of issues	4	0	1	0
Moody's Investor Service				
Rating	Aaa	Aa1-3	A1-3	Baa1-3
No. of issues	26	7	1	0
Standard & Poor's				
Rating*	AAA	AA	A	BBB
No. of issues	22	5	2	0

---

*Fitch Investor Service uses the same rating scale as S&P.

Sources: *Asset Sales Report* and Duff & Phelps.

In analyzing the structure, the agencies look at the credit risk, the cash flows, and legal issues. Credit risk analysis includes, first, assessing the orginator's overall risk profile; second, assessing the portfolio quality and characteristics (e.g., term to maturity, seasoning, and geographic distribution of assets in the portfolio), the pool selection process, and the originator's credit and underwriting practices; and third, evaluating the servicer and the trustee. The servicer's staffing, experience, efficiency, and accounting and auditing procedures are reviewed, along with the trustee's responsibilities, financial condition, and experience as a trustee.

Cash flow analysis consists of looking for specific risk inherent in the payment structure and collateral. For example, a pay-through structure will carry reinvestment risk if the payments on the collaterized notes occur less frequently than payments on the collateral and if it is likely that the funds cannot be reinvested between payment dates in assets that yield a rate at least as high as the highest rate to be paid on the collateralized notes.

An analysis of the legal issues includes an examination of the perfection of lien or asset ownership and an evaluation of the risks associated with the possible bankruptcy of the seller and servicer. Because the legal and credit issues are interrelated, legal issues are mitigated if the originator/servicer's credit quality is high.

The credit enhancement and credit enhancer are crucial to the rating of an issue. The level of credit enhancement, as well as the credit quality of the credit enhancer, is evaluated by the rating agency when the credit enhancer is a third-party. An issue can be rated no higher than the credit rating of the credit enhancer. An issue, however, can be rated lower than the credit enhancer's rating if the level of credit enhancement is judged insufficient by the rating agency. Adequate credit enhancement is usually several times the historical default rate and should reflect the amount and timing of potential losses and provide a cushion to reflect uncertainty about the statistical validity of applying analysis of the originator's entire portfolio to a possibly less diversified pool.

Once a public issue has been rated by a credit rating agency, the agency monitors the issue regularly throughout the life of the issue for possible rating changes. An issue can be downgraded or upgraded. Since most asset-backed securities, however, are initially rated AAA/Aaa/D&P-1, downgrades are more common than upgrades. Rating changes result from changes in the credit quality of the credit enhancer or from changes in the credit quality of the assets securitized. If the assets perform poorly, the credit enhancement will be drawn down more rapidly than the assets amortize and the level of credit enhancement will fall to an inadequate level, resulting in a rating downgrade. As of June 1988, less than 10 asset-backed securities issues had been downgraded.

Trustees

A trustee in an asset-backed securities issue is the intermediary between the servicer and investors and between the credit enhancer and the investors. A trustee is used in an asset-backed securities issue whether that issue be a sale of assets by the issuer or a collateralized debt obligation of the issuer.

According to the Trust Indenture Act of 1939, a bond trustee for debt offerings in excess of $1 million must be an insured depository institution with minimum capitalization of $50,000. Standard & Poor's, however, requires that the trustee have at least $500 million of capital, and as of December 1987, all trustees for asset-backed securities have been commercial banks with at least $500 million of capital. As shown in Table 2-8, nine commercial banks act as trustee for nearly every publicly sold issue of nonmortgage-related asset-backed securities. The responsibilities of trustees include buying the assets from the issuer on behalf of the trust and issuing certificates to the investors. As the obligors make principal and interest payments on the assets, the servicer deposits the proceeds in the trust account, and the trustee passes them on to the investors. If the funds are not immediately passed through to the investors, the trustee may be responsible for reinvesting the funds. Trustees are also responsible for determining the sufficiency of the various reports made by the servicer to the investors and for passing the reports on to the investors. Finally, the trustee should be willing and able to take over the servicer's role if the servicer withdraws or is unable to perform.

The trust is established by the issuer and the trustee. It consists of a pool of assets, usually loans, and includes all rights to receive payments due on those loans, security interests in the collateral securing those loans, and certain insurance, including the credit enhancement.

There are two basic types of trust—the grantor trust and the owner trust. The sale of assets to either type of trust constitutes a true sale of assets for the issuer of the asset-backed securities. The major distinctions between the two types of trusts lie in the tax treatment and the type of security issued by the trusts.

**Table 2-8   Trustees of Asset-Backed Securities
1987–Public Issues**

Trustee	$Millions	Number of Issues
Fuji Bank	$2,248.2	4
State Street Bank	1,806.5	6
Bank of New York	1,674.8	4
Manufacturers Hanover	1,600.0	4
Morgan Guaranty	815.6	4
First National Bank of Chicago	784.2	2
Bankers Trust	637.3	6
Chemical Bank	542.6	3
First Bank	183.5	2

Source: IDD Information Services and SEC filings.

A grantor trust is a trust in which the certificate holders are treated as beneficial owners of the assets sold. The net income from the trust is taxed on a pass-through basis as if the certificate holders actually owned an interest in the receivables. To qualify for the grantor trust, the structure of the deal must be passive; that is, the trust cannot be a vehicle for engaging in profitable activities for the investors. This criterion is usually satisfied by establishment of a fixed pool of assets. There can be only limited, if any, substitution of assets, and reinvestment is limited to that between payment dates.

An owner trust is considered a partnership for tax purposes. The owner of the trust is the issuer of the asset-backed securities. The interest paid by the obligors and the interest paid to the investors is recognized on the issuer's financial statements as interest income and interest expense. The certificates issued by the owner trust represent a debt obligation of the trust collateralized by the assets sold to the trust, rather than ownership of the assets in the trust. The owner trust is used when the cash flows from the underlying assets do not perfectly match the payments made to investors.

Structures

As stated earlier, not every player and not every piece discussed in this chapter is involved in every asset-backed security issue. This section, however, discusses how many of the pieces and players come together by decribing two "typical" issues—the first structured as interest in a pool of assets and the second as collateralized debt.

Pass-Throughs

Figure 2-1 illustrates the sale of assets through a pass-through structure. The originator sells the assets to a grantor trust. The trustee, then, on behalf of the trust, issues certificates to the investors. Each certificate represents an undivided interest in the

**Figure 2-1   A "Typical" Asset-Backed Securities Issue
Structured as a Pass-Through**

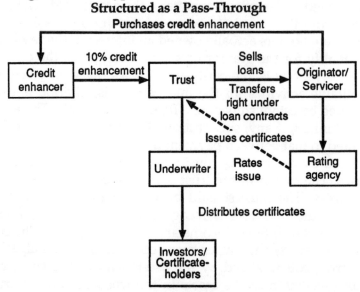

entire portfolio of loans. Along with the loans, the originator conveys to the trust for the benefit of the investors, all rights, title, and interest in the assets and all rights to receive payments due under insurance policies covering individual loan contracts and under the insurance provided by the credit enhancer.

The credit enhancement, an insurance bond purchased by the originator, covers some proportion of the dollar amount of the underlying assets at the date of issue—in this example, the proportion is 10 percent. This level of credit enhancement was primarily determined by the credit rating agency, which required at least that amount of credit enhancement for the rating desired by the originator.

The credit enhancement up to the first payment date is equal to 10 percent of the underlying assets. Thereafter, it is reduced by payments made by the insurer to cover delinquencies and defaults. Defaulted contracts are, in effect, purchased by the credit enhancer, and all rights under those contracts are assigned to the credit enhancer. Any payments made on defaulted contracts are reimbursed to the credit enhancer, but any late fees remain with the servicer. If the amount of credit enhancement is reduced to zero, the investors bear all credit risk remaining.

The investors, trustee, and credit enhancer have no recourse to the originator unless the originator breaches its warranty that each loan contract complies with all requirements of law or breaches its warranties relating to the validity, subsistence, perfection and priority of the interest in the collateral securing each loan contract. A breach of any of these warranties that adversely affects any loan contract could obligate the originator to repurchase that contract or correct the breach.

Figure 2-2 illustrates the cash flows in a typical pass-through structure. The payments by the obligors are paid into a separate interest-bearing account maintained in the trust department of an insured bank (the trustee) in the name of the trustee. This account is known as the collection account. Payments into this account are applied first to pay monthly principal and interest to certificate-holders and second to pay the monthly fee to the servicer for servicing and acting as custodian of original loan contracts and other documents relating to contracts. On each payment date the trustee passes along monthly principal and interest payments to investors. The originator is responsible for paying the trustee's fee and the insurance bond fee. Under the insurance bond, the trust is entitled to require payment from insurer to collection account to cover payment delinquencies and defaults. These payments are reimbursable to the insurer from the collection account to the extent repaid by the obligors.

Asset-Backed Bonds

The cash flows and structure of an asset-backed bond issue, which involves the issuance of collateralized debt by the originator of the underlying assets, are very similar to the cash flows and structure of an issue that involves the sale of assets.

**Figure 2-2   Cash Flows of a "Typical" Asset-Backed
Securities Issue Structured as a Sale of Assets (Pass-Through)**

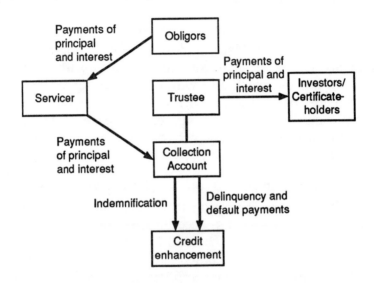

As shown in Figure 2-3, the primary difference is that the originator sells the assets to a wholly-owned subsidiary created for the sole purpose of securitizing the assets. The assets, therefore, remain on the originator's consolidated balance sheet. The subsidiary does not sell the assets to a trust that issues certificates or notes to investors. Rather, the subsidiary itself issues general obligation notes to investors, which are in fact collateralized by the subsidiary's sole assets, namely, those sold to it by the originator of the issue.

The use of a debt structure rather than a sale structure as well as modifications of those two basic structures varies according to the type of issuer, the type of assets securitized, and the legal, regulatory, accounting, and tax environment in which the issuer operates. The following chapters examine these topics in more detail.

Figure 2-3 A "Typical" Asset-Backed Securities Issue Structured as a Collateralized Debt

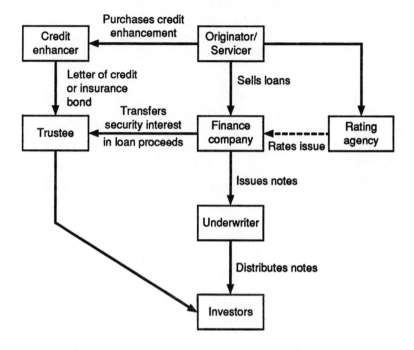

PART II
▶ Asset-Backed ◀
Securities

CHAPTER 3

▶ Mortgage-Backed ◀ Securities

RESIDENTIAL MORTGAGE LOANS were the first type of loan to be securitized. Although many other types of loans have been securitized recently, residential mortgage loans still account for the bulk of asset-backed securities. During 1987, $323 billion of residential mortgage-backed securities were issued publicly. This is over 30 times the amount of securities backed by non-mortgage loans that were issued that year.

Volumes have been written on nearly every facet of mortgage-backed securities.[1] This chapter, therefore, makes no attempt to exhaustively discuss such securities. Instead, the purpose of this chapter is to give an overview of mortgage-backed securities by discussing the characteristics of mortgage loans, the primary market for such loans, the characteristics of the most common types of mortgage-backed securities, and their risks and returns.

---

1 See, for example, *The Handbook of Mortgage-Backed Securities,* Probus Publishing (1987) and *The Handbook of Mortgage Banking: A Guide to the Secondary Mortgage Market,* Dow Jones-Irwin (1985).

Table 3-1   Amortization Schedule for a Fixed-Rate Mortgage Loan (30-year, 10 percent APR, $50,000)

Month	Payment	Principal	Interest	Balance
0	0	0	0	$50,000.00
1	$438.79	$22.12	$416.67	49,977.88
2	438.79	22.31	416.48	49,955.57
3	438.79	22.41	416.30	49,910.40
4	438.79	22.68	416.11	49,887.53
12	438.79	24.24	414.55	49,722.01
60	438.79	36.10	402.69	48,286.84
120	438.79	59.39	379.40	45,468.19
180	438.79	97.72	341.07	40,830.60
240	438.79	160.78	278.01	33,200.35
300	478.79	264.53	174.26	20,646.00
360	478.79	426.05	3.55	0.00

Because the majority of mortgage-backed securities are collateralized by residential mortgage loans, this chapter will concentrate on those types of loans and securities backed by them. A brief discussion of commercial mortgage loans is provided in the last section of this chapter.

Mortgage Loans

A mortgage is a pledge of property to secure payment of a debt. For residential mortgages, the property is usually a house and the land on which it is built, and the debt is a loan to purchase the house and land. A borrower, known as the "mortgagor," borrows the funds to purchase property in exchange for a pledge to relinquish the property to the lender, known as the "mortgagee," should the borrower default.

Types of Residential Mortgages

There are many types of residential mortgage loans, but three are most common. These three are the fixed-rate, graduated-payment, and adjustable-rate mortgages. As shown in Figure 3-1, most mortgage-backed securities are collateralized by fixed-rate mortgage loans.

Fixed-rate loans are level-pay, self-amoritizing loans that require monthly payment usually over a 30-year period. Table 3-1 illustrates the payment and amortization schedule for a $50,000 fixed-rate, 30-year mortgage at a 10-percent annual

Figure 3-1 Types of Residential Mortgage Loans that Back Single-Family Agency Pass-Throughs (as June 1987)

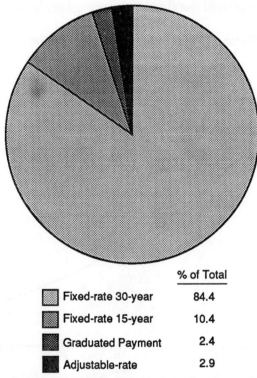

		% of Total
▨	Fixed-rate 30-year	84.4
▨	Fixed-rate 15-year	10.4
▨	Graduated Payment	2.4
▉	Adjustable-rate	2.9

Source: "Introduction to Mortgages and Mortgage-Backed Securities," Salomon Brothers, Inc., September 1987.

percentage rate. As shown in this table, in the early years of the mortgage, nearly all of the monthly payments are devoted to interest, and in the later years nearly all of the monthly payments are devoted to principal.

Also, as illustrated in Figure 3-2, over the life of a mortgage loan, interest accounts for a much larger proportion of total payments than does principal. At the end of the first year of the loan in Figure 3-2, total interest payments will be nearly 18 times total principal payments. At the end of 30 years, when the loan is completely repaid, total interest payments made will be more than twice the total amount borrowed.

A second common type of residential mortgage loan is the graduated-payment mortgage (GPM). This type of mortgage loan is a variation of the fixed-rate mortgage. It was developed

Figure 3-2   Ratio of Total Interest to Principal Payments over the Life of a Fixed-Rate Mortgage Loan

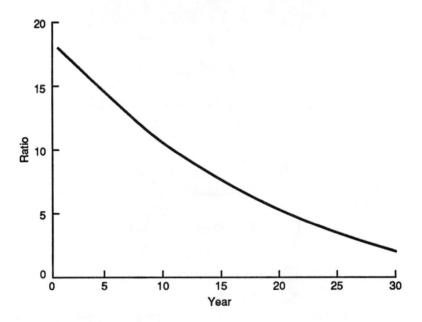

in the late 1970s when high interest rates made it difficult for young, first-time home buyers to qualify for fixed-rate mortgage loans. The GPM provides for increasing monthly payments over the first few years of the life of the loan. Thereafter, payments are level. The actual number of years over which payments rise and the percentage increase per year depends on the type of GPM. The most common type is a 30-year mortgage loan in which payments rise by 7.5 percent for the first five years. During the first years when payments are increasing, the monthly payments do not cover the interest due on the loan. The interest accrues and is added to the principal balance. This is called negative amortization. After the period of increasing payments, the level monthly payments are based on the existing principal balance. Figure 3-3, illustrates the payment and amortization schedules of the most common GPM.

Figure 3-3 Monthly Payment Schedule for Graduated Payment Mortgage ($50,000, 30-year, 10 percent APR)

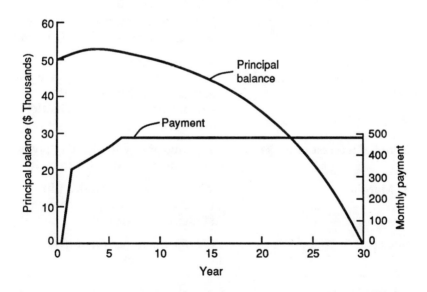

Source: Dexter Senft, "Mortgages," Chapter 2, *The Handbook of Mortgage-Backed Securities*, Frank Fabozzi, ed., (Chicago, IL: Probus Publishing, 1988).

A third common type of mortgage is the adjustable-rate mortgage (ARM). This type of loan also has its origins in the high interest rate environment of the late 1970s and early 1980s. An ARM differs from a fixed-rate mortgage and a GPM in that the interest rate on an ARM is reset periodically.

While there are many different types of ARM contracts, they share a number of common features (see Table 3-2). All ARMs stipulate the frequency of adjustment, most commonly once per year. ARM contracts also specify an index of adjustment, which usually coincides with the frequency of adjustment. For example, a common index for an ARM that adjusts every year is the rate on a one-year Treasury note. ARM contracts also specify the initial interest rate. Sometimes, to attract

Table 3-2   Common Features of Adjustable Rate Mortgages

Common Feature	*Comments*
1. Frequency of adjustment	Most common interval is one year; also common are one and six months and three and five years.
2. Index of adjustment	One-year Treasury rate, and weighted average cost of funds for 11th Federal Home Loan Bank District are common.
3. Initial interest rate	Discounts or buydowns may push initial rate below the risk-free rate.
4. Margin	Adjusted rate equals index plus margin or inital rate plus change in index of adjustment.
5. Caps	Per adjustment period or over life of loan or both.

Source: *The Handbook of Mortgage-Backed Securities.* Frank Fabozzi, ed., (Chicago, IL: Probus Publishing, 1987).

borrowers, this rate is below the rate on a Treasury security of comparable maturity. Another feature common to all ARMs is that they specify a margin by which the interest rate adjusts. The interest rate on the loan might be specified as the index plus the margin or the initial rate plus the change in the index. ARMs also include interest-rate caps to protect borrowers against wide swings in interest rates. Caps can be specified per adjustment period, over the life of the loan, or both.

Origination Standards

As types of mortgage loans vary, so do origination standards. They vary by type of mortgage as well as by lender. Nevertheless, a few common features exist. First, total monthly mortgage payments (principal and interest) should not exceed 25 percent of the borrower's adjusted monthly gross income (gross income less any payments owed to other creditors). Second, total mortgage payments plus other housing expenses should be less than 33 percent of adjusted gross income. Third, downpayments usually must be between five and 25 percent of the appraised value of the property mortgaged. The first two underwriting requirements are to ensure that the borrower can repay his debt; the third requirement is to give the borrower the proper incentive to make his debt payments. The third requirement also provides a cushion to the lender should he have to foreclose and sell the property at less than the originally appraised value.

As an added protection, lenders usually require borrowers to pay for private mortgage insurance (PMI) if the downpayment on a conventional loan is less than 20 percent of the appraised value of the mortgaged property. PMI covers some percentage of the loan amount should the borrower default. In the event of default, the private insurer would either pay the lender that percentage or would pay off the entire principal balance and take title of the mortgaged property.

The Primary Market for Mortgage Loans

At year-end 1987, $2.9 trillion of mortgage loans were outstanding. Nearly, $1.9 trillion, 65 percent, represented residential mortgages. As shown in Figure 3-4, the remaining 35 percent was in commercial, multifamily, and farm mortgage loans.

Figure 3-4   Types of Mortgage Loans Outstanding: Year-end 1987

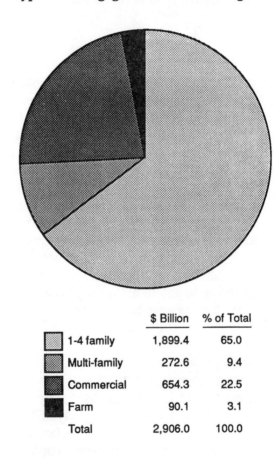

		$ Billion	% of Total
	1-4 family	1,899.4	65.0
	Multi-family	272.6	9.4
	Commercial	654.3	22.5
	Farm	90.1	3.1
	Total	2,906.0	100.0

Source: Board of Governors of the Federal Reserve System.

The primary players in the residential mortgage market are thrift institutions—savings and loan associations and savings banks. Thrifts were originally organized in the mid-1800s as cooperatives to finance the home purchases of their members. As demand for homes increased, thrifts expanded by accepting deposits and offering loans to nonmembers. Today, thrifts are still primarily residential mortgage lenders. They are encouraged by regulatory and tax considerations to hold residential mortgage loans, which they fund mostly with short-term time deposits.

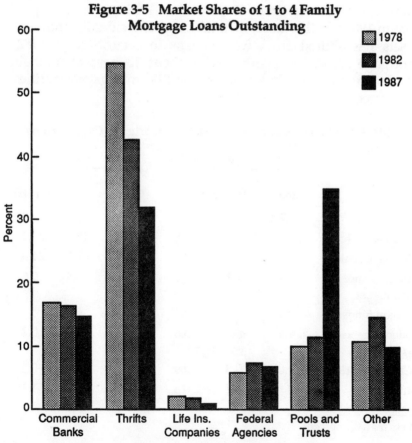

Figure 3-5 Market Shares of 1 to 4 Family Mortgage Loans Outstanding

Source: Board of Governors of the Federal Reserve System.

Deregulation, which has allowed thrifts to expand beyond residential mortgage lending, has changed the role of thrifts in the mortgage market. In 1982, thrifts originated about 40 percent of all residential mortgage loans; this compares with 46 percent in 1987 (Table 3-3). In 1982, they held over 40 percent of all 1-4 residential mortgage loans and about 40 percent all mortgage pass-through securities (Figure 3-5). In 1987, however, they held only 32 percent of residential mortgage loans outstanding, and about 30 percent of all mortgage-backed securities. Consequently, S&Ls have decreased their share of total residential mortgage loans outstanding (whole loans and mortgage securities) from 42 percent in 1982 to about 31 percent in 1987. Furthermore, their holdings of residential mortage assets has shifted from whole loans to securities. In 1982, mortgage securities accounted for about 13 percent of their residential mortgage holdings, but by 1987 mortgage securities accounted for nearly 25 percent.

Table 3-3   Market Shares of 1-4 Family Mortgage Originations

	1982			1987		
	Conv.	FHA/VA	Total	Conv.	FHA/VA	Total
Thrifts	48.7%	4.8%	39.7%	53.6%	10.2%	46.3%
Commercial banks	29.9	9.7	25.8	28.3	15.5	26.2
Mortgage banks	15.5	80.6	28.7	15.6	69.9	24.8
Life insurance companies	0.4	1.3	0.6	0.6	0.6	0.6
Pension funds	0.1	0	0.1	*	0	*
Federal agencies	4.5	0	3.6	0.8	0	0.7
State & local Credit agencies	1.0	0.3	0.9	0.2	0.2	0.2
Builders	0	3.2	0.6	0.9	3.5	1.3

*Less than 0.1 percent

Source: Federal Home Loan Mortgage Corporation.

Figure 3-6 Shares of Mortgage Loans Sold: 1987

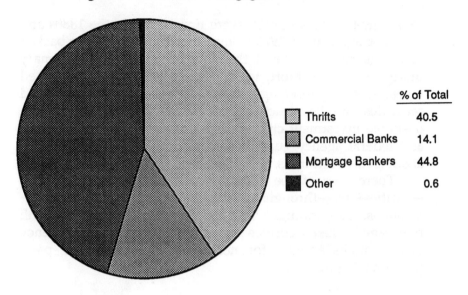

	% of Total
☐ Thrifts	40.5
▨ Commercial Banks	14.1
▧ Mortgage Bankers	44.8
■ Other	0.6

Source: Secondary Mortgage Markets.

Securitization seems to have played an important part in thrifts' changing role in residential mortgage lending, and it has enabled them to originate a larger share of mortgage loans by freeing them of the risks of funding the loans. Thrifts sold 35 percent of all mortgage loans that they acquired either through originations or purchases. Furthermore, they accounted for over 40 percent of all mortgage loans sold in 1987 (see Figure 3-6).

Unlike thrifts, mortgage bankers sell nearly all of the loans that they originate. In 1987, they accounted for 45 percent of the dollar amount of mortgage loans sold. The importance of mortgage bankers in the residential mortgage market has increased since the 1970s due to the development of an active secondary mortgage market. Historically, they concentrated on FHA/VA loans, and today originate over 70 percent of such mortgage loans. Their share, however, has fallen since 1982.

Mortgage-Backed Securities

Mortgage-backed securities were first issued in the 1880s and then not again until 1970.[2] Since that time, mortgage-backed securities have facilitated the flow of funds to the primary mortgage market. Mortgage-backed securities have increased investment in mortgage loans because mortgage-backed securities can be structured to eliminate some of the undesirable investment characteristics of whole mortgage loans, and federal agency guarantees considerably reduce concerns about creditworthiness.

There are three basic types of mortgage-backed securities—pass-throughs, mortgage-backed bonds, and pay-throughs. Pass-throughs account for over two-thirds of all mortgage-backed securities issued in 1987, and federal agency pass-throughs account for nearly all publicly issued pass-throughs (Figure 3-7).

Pass-Throughs

A pass-through represents direct ownership in a portfolio of mortgage loans. The portfolio is placed in trust, and certificates of ownership are sold to investors. The originator usually services the loans and collects interest and principal, passing them on, less a servicing fee, to the investors.

The growth in the securitization of mortgage loans via pass-throughs has been rapid. Figure 3-8 indicates that mortgage pass-through securities have been growing faster than the overall market for taxable, fixed-income securities. In 1976, such mortgage pass-throughs represented only four percent of all taxable, fixed-income securities; in 1986, they accounted for 16 percent of such securities.

---

2 Bonds collateralized by pools of mortgage loans held in trusts were first issued in the 1880s. The practice ended, however, during the depression of the 1890s. See Alan G. Bogue, *Money and Interest*, (University of Nebraska Press, 1955.)

Figure 3-7   Issuance of Mortgage-Backed Securities by Type: 1987

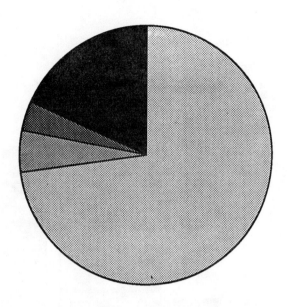

		% of Total
▨	Pass-through agency	72.8
▨	Pass-through private	5.2
▨	Morgage-backed bond	3.7
■	Multi-class/CMO	18.3

Source: Secondary Mortgage Markets.

Figure 3-8 Taxable Fixed-Income Securites Amount Outstanding at Year-End

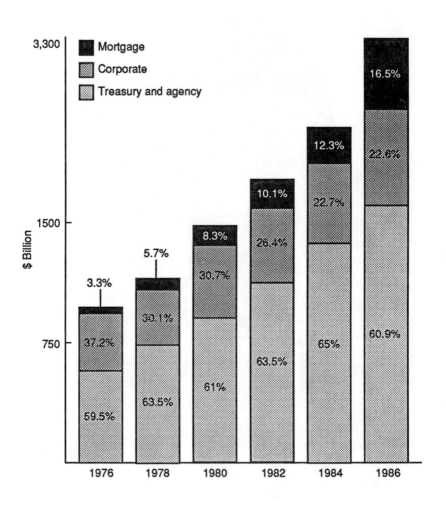

*Excludes mortgage securites issued by Federal agencies.

Source: Board of Governors of the Federal Reserve System.

Table 3-4 Mortgage Pass-Through Securities and Home Mortgage Loans Outstanding ($ Billions)

Mortgage Pass-Throughs	1980	1982	1984	1986	1987
GNMAs	$91.6	$115.8	$175.6	$256.9	$311.6
Freddie Mac PCs	13.5	42.6	70.3	166.7	205.6
FNMA MBSs	NA	14.5	36.0	95.8	138.0
Private Sector*	1.3	1.7	3.6	8.0	17.0
Total	103.4	174.6	285.5	527.4	672.2
Residential Mortgage Loans	987.0	1,105.7	1,318.5	1,666.4	1,889.4
Pass-Throughs as a Percent of Residential Mortgage Loans	10.5%	15.8%	21.7%	31.5%	35.6%

*Public offerings; 1987 estimated.

Sources: Board of Governors of the Federal Reserve System and Salomon Brothers, "Securitization and the Mortgage Market," August 1987.

The total dollar volume of federal agency mortgage pass-throughs outstanding in 1987 was over six times the amount outstanding at the end of 1980 and represented over 35 percent of all residential mortgages outstanding in 1987 (see Table 3-4).

Federal agency pass-throughs, issued by the Government National Mortgage Association, Federal National Mortgage Association, and Federal Home Loan Mortgage Corporation, are all very similar, but there are some important distinctions (Table 3-5). First, GNMA securities are backed only by FHA/VA loans, while FNMA and FHLMC securities are backed mainly by conventional mortgage loans. Second, Ginnie Mae is not the issuer of GNMA securities. Rather, GNMA-

Table 3-5   Comparison of Federal Agency Pass-Throughs

	Government National Mortgage Corporation	Federal National Mortgage Corporation	Federal Home Loan Mortgage Corporation
Issuer	FHA/VA-approved lenders	FNMA	FHLMC
Underlying Assets	FHA/VA mortgage loans	Conventional or FHA/VA mortgage loans	Conventional or FHA/VA mortgage loans
Guarantee	Full and timely payment of principal and interest	Full and timely payment of principal and interest	Full and timely payment of interest or full and timely payment of principal and interest

Source: Salomon Brothers.

approved issuers originate, pool and place mortgage loans in trusts. These issuers then, upon receiving Ginnie Mae's approval, issue GNMA-guaranteed pass-through securities. Both Fannie Mae and Freddie Mac purchase uninsured or privately insured mortgage loans from originators and issue the pass-through securities themselves. Fannie Mae and Freddie Mac often have some recourse to the originators. A third difference among the federal mortgage agencies is that Ginnie Mae requires much more homogeneity for the pools that back up its securities than do Fannie Mae and Freddie Mac. Ginnie Mae requires that a pool consist of only one type of recently originated loans with similar interest rate and maturity, while Fannie Mae and Freddie Mac allow a pool to consist of seasoned loans of varying interest rates. Finally, the nature of the three agencies' guarantees can vary. Ginnie Mae and Fannie Mae guarantee the timely payment of principal and inter-

Figure 3-9 Shares of Agency Pass-Throughs Outstanding

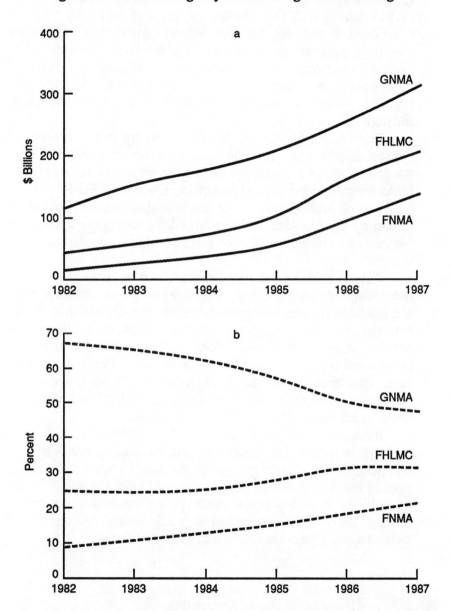

Source: Board of Governors of the Federal Reserve System.

est, while Freddie Mac guarantees the timely payment of interest but usually only the ultimate payment of principal.

GNMAs account for the largest proportion of agency mortgage pass-throughs outstanding, but their proportion has declined over time. In 1987 GNMAs constituted 48 percent of mortgage pass-throughs, down from 66 percent in 1982, the first full year that all three federal agencies issued pass-throughs (Figure 3-9).

One reason for Ginnie Mae's lost share is the success of Fannie Mae's and Freddie Mac's swap programs. These programs allow a mortgage lender to swap whole mortgage loans for mortgage-backed securities. Over the 1982-87 period, between 68 and 94 percent of the mortgage-backed securities issued by Fannie Mae were swapped for mortgage loans, and between 58 and 90 percent of Freddie Mac's new issues were swaps.[3]

Private sector pass-throughs are not as common as the federal agency pass-throughs because private securities are not a substitute for agency pass-throughs but an alternative for conventional mortgage loans that do not conform to the criteria of the federal agencies. Most mortgage loans that are securitized conform to the federal agencies' criteria and, therefore, are securitized as FNMA and FHLMC securities. Mortgage loans that do not conform are either held as whole loans or are securitized in the private sector.

Bank of America issued the first private sector pass-through in 1977. The securities were backed by conventional mortgages, and private mortgage insurance covered the entire pool of loans rather than each individual loan. Only $17 billion in publicly issued private sector pass-throughs were issued during 1987.[4] This amounted to only seven percent of all federal agency pass-throughs issued at that time.

---

3 Federal Home Loan Mortgage Corporation.

4 Federal Home Loan Mortgage Corporation.

Mortgage-Backed Bonds

The second type of mortgage-backed security is the mortgage-backed bond (MBB). Like the pass-through, the MBB is collateralized by a portfolio of mortgages. Sometimes an MBB is backed by a portfolio of mortgage pass-through securities such as GNMAs. Unlike the pass-through, the MBB is a debt obligation of the issuer, so the portfolio of mortgages used as collateral remain on the issuer's books as assets and the mortgage-backed bonds are reported as liabilities. Also, the cash flows from the collateral are not dedicated to the payment of principal and interest on mortgage-backed securities. Mortgage-backed bonds have a stated maturity (usually between five and 12 years). Interest is generally paid semiannually, and principal is paid at maturity.

One important characteristic of mortgage-backed bonds is that they are usually overcollateralized. The collateral is evaluated quarterly, and if its value falls below the amount stated in the bond indenture, more mortgage loans or securities must be added to the collateral.

Both the private sector and federal agencies issue mortgage-backed bonds, although they are much more prevalent among private issues. In the private sector, they are issued by savings and loan associations and mutual savings banks. The number of issues, however, has been limited. In 1987, only about $12 billion of mortgage-backed bonds were issued.[5] This is less than five percent of the pass-throughs issued. One reason for this limited activity is that mortgage-backed securities may be more costly to issue than pass-throughs. Because the mortgages that serve as collateral remain on the issuer's books, a depository institution that issues mortgage-backed securities must cover these loans with a certain proportion of capital. Also, the institution may have to hold non-interest-bearing reserves with the Federal Reserve against the proceeds.[6]

5 Federal Home Loan Mortgage Corporation.

6 See Chapter 7 for a more detailed discussion of reserve requirements.

Pay-Throughs

The third type of mortgage-backed security is the pay-through bond. This bond combines some of the features of the pass-through with some of those of the mortgage-backed bond. The bond is collateralized by a pool of assets and appears on the issuer's financial statements as debt. The cash flows from the assets, however, are dedicated to servicing the bonds in a way similar to that of pass-throughs.

In June 1983, Freddie Mac issued a pay-through bond known as the CMO (collateralized mortgage obligation). Each CMO issue was divided into three maturity classes, and each class received semiannual interest payments. Class 1 bondholders, however, received the first installments of principal payments and any prepayments until Class 1 bonds were paid off. Class 2 bondholders, in turn, received principal payments and prepayments before Class 3 bondholders received any principal payments. The original Freddie Mac CMO was structured so that Class 1 bonds were repaid within five years of the offering date; Class 2 bonds, within 12 years; and Class 3, within 20 years.

Since Freddie Mac developed the first CMO, multi-class pay-throughs have become the most popular type of pay-throughs issued, and many variations have been developed. Issues of CMOs now have from three to more than six maturity classes. Most CMO issues, however, have four "regular" maturity classes and a "residual" class. The first three classes pay interest at stated rates beginning with the issue date. The fourth class, known as the "Z class," is an accrual bond. That is, earned interest accrues to the principal balance and is therefore compounded while the other classes are receiving principal and interest. After the first three classes are repaid, the Z class receives regular interest and principal payments along with accrued interest.

The residual class receives the remaining cash flows from the underlying mortgages after the regular classes are repaid. Residual income arises because the total cash flows generated from the underlying assets are expected to exceed payments to the regular class bondholders. Excess income will also be generated from temporary reinvestment of cash flows pending transfers to regular bondholders.

In addition to Freddie Mac, private sector firms also issue pay-throughs. As shown in Table 3-6, at least five different types of private firms issue CMOs. Private conduits, which include investment banks, account for the greatest dollar amount of CMOs issued—$96.3 billion, 58.4 percent, as of 1986.

Table 3-6 CMO Issuers: 1983 to 1987

Issuer	$millions	% of Total
Private conduits*	$96,329	58.4%
Federal agencies	34,984	21.2
Builders	23,430	14.2
Thrift institutions	9,552	5.8
Other	660	0.4

*Includes private thrift conduits.

Source: Federal Home Loan Mortgage Corporation.

The activity in pay-throughs has been growing rapidly (see Figure 3-10). Total dollar volume of CMOs was only $4.7 billion in 1983, but was more than 12 times that in 1987. Nevertheless, CMO issuance is dwarfed by pass-throughs. Furthermore, pass-throughs serve as collateral for nearly 90 percent of CMOs issued since 1983 (see Figure 3-11). Conventional mortgages are collateral for nine percent of CMOs issued, and a mixture of conventional mortgages and pass-throughs account for the remainder.

Figure 3-10   Issuance of CMOs: 1983–1987 (Public offerings)

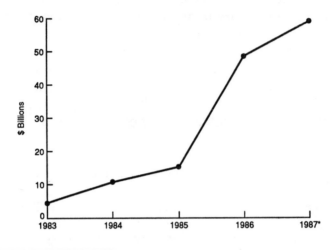

*1987 includes some other multi-class mortgage securities.

Source: Federal Home Loan Mortgage Corporation.

Banks and thrifts are also the primary purchasers of the residual classes. Because residual income is inversely related to prepayment rates, banks and thrifts use the residual bonds as hedging vehicles. In periods of rising interest rates, when the market value of existing low-rate mortgages are falling, prepayment rates are low and the returns on the residual class of bonds are increasing.

Table 3-7   Major Investors of CMOs: 1986

Maturity Class (weighted average maturity)	Thrift Institutions	Commercial Banks	Insurance Companies	Pension Funds	Other
Class 1 (Less than 4 years)	8.7%	24.3%	11.2%	44.5%	11.3%
Class 2 (4.1 to 7 years)	13.0	21.0	19.3	39.0	7.7
Class 3 (7.1 to 10 years)	5.2	5.8	20.9	56.0	12.1
Class 4 (More than 10 years)	10.2	0.5	21.8	46.0	21.5

Source: Salomon Brothers, "Securitization and the Mortgage Market," August 1987.

Figure 3-11   Collateral of CMOs Issued from 1983 to 1987

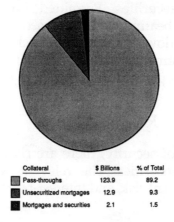

Collateral	$ Billions	% of Total
Pass-throughs	123.9	89.2
Unsecuritized mortgages	12.9	9.3
Mortgages and securities	2.1	1.5

Source: Federal Home Loan Mortgage Corporation.

REMICS

As mentioned above, CMOs are structured as debt obligations rather than true asset sales. This was done to comply with tax regulations, which stated that a trust generally could not qualify for grantor trust status if it issues multi-class interests that divide ownership of investment assets or the cash flows from such assets in a non-pro rata fashion. As a consequence of their status as debt instruments, certain "inefficiencies," such as a minimum capital requirement, had to be built into CMO structures. The issuance of CMOs was therefore limited. The Tax Reform Act of 1986, however, eliminated many of the structural inefficiencies of CMOs by authorizing REMICs—real estate mortgage investment conduits.

REMICs are very similar to CMOs but differ in one important respect—tax treatment. REMICs can qualify as asset sales for tax purposes if the following conditions are met. First, a REMIC must contain at least one regular class and only one residual class. Second, the collateral of a REMIC must consist of "qualified mortgages" or "permitted investments." Qualified mortgages would include single- and multi-family residential mortgage loans and commercial mortgages as well as mortgage-backed securities. Permitted investments include short-term interest-bearing securities used solely for reinvesting monthly cash flows pending their scheduled transfer to bondholders; investments to fund operating expenses of the REMIC; and real property acquired through foreclosure.

Risks and Returns

As with any type of security, there are risks associated with mortgage-backed securities. The relevant types of risk are credit risk, prepayment risk, and interest-rate risk.

Credit Risk

Credit risk is the risk of default. With mortgage-backed securities it is also the risk that the cash flows from the underlying mortgage loans will not support the timely payment of principal and interest due on the securities. Credit risk is generally not a major concern for most mortgage-backed securities issued. That is, credit quality is not important for federal agency pass-throughs and for mortgage-backed bonds and pay-throughs collateralized by federal agency mortgage securities. Ginnie Mae, Fannie Mae, and Freddie Mac guarantee the payment of principal and interest on their securities. Ginnie Mae has the full faith and support of the U. S. government, and Fannie Mae and Freddie Mac are closely tied to the U.S. government.[7]

---

7 The Department of the Treasury and Housing and Urban Development have some regulatory authority over Fannie Mae; the Treasury may extend credit to the organization; and one-third of its directors are appointed by the president of the United States. Freddie Mac's board consists of three members of the Federal Home Loan Bank Board, who are appointed by the president of the United States, and the board has the authority to require the Federal Home Loan Banks to guarantee the obligations of Freddie Mac. For more detail, see Kenneth J. Thygerson, "Federal-Government Related Mortgage Purchasers," in *The Handbook of Mortgage Banking: A Guide to the Secondary Mortgage Market*, (Dow Jones-Irwin, 1985.)

Credit risk is, however, an issue for private mortgage-backed securities. In assessing the credit quality of a pool of mortgage loans, Standard & Poor's has identified some key factors that affect credit quality (see Table 3-8). With respect to these factors, Standard & Poor's defines a prime pool of mortgage loans as a pool of at least 300 individual fixed-rate, fully amortizing, level-pay, first mortgage loans of less than $300,000 each. These loans were made to finance the purchase of owner-occupied, single-family, detached one-unit residences. The loans should have a loan-to-value ratio of 80 percent or less, and no more than five percent of the loans should be from any single ZIP code. According to Standard & Poor's, the "loss coverage," i.e., the level of credit enhancement, on such a prime pool should be seven percent for an AAA rating, four percent for an AA, and 2.8 percent for an A.

Prepayment Risk

The rating agencies do not analyze prepayment risk, and therefore it is not factored into their ratings. Prepayment risk is the risk that the obligors of the underlying mortgage loans prepay their loans at a greater than expected rate and therefore reduce the yield on the securities. Prepayment risk is a primary concern of investors in and issuers of mortgage-backed securities.

The value of a security is the discounted present value of its cash flows. When the cash flows are certain, the value is fairly straightforward and easy to calculate, but when the cash flows are uncertain, determining the value is more difficult. Because mortgage loans include a call option—an option to prepay—the cash flows from mortgage loans are uncertain.

This uncertainty leads to prepayment risk, which is of concern to investors and some issuers of mortgage-backed securities. Prepayment affects the yield and the actual life of mortgage pass-throughs. Also, prepayment may leave investors unexpectedly with funds to invest, at possibly lower rates. Similarly, faster than expected prepayment may expose issuers of mortgage-backed bonds and CMOs to reinvestment risk. If underlying mortgage loans prepay faster than scheduled, issuers may have to reinvest the cash flows, possibly at rates lower than the coupons on the mortgage-backed debt.

Table 3-8 Key Determinants of a Mortgage Pool's Credit Risk

Factor	*Comments*
1. Loan-to-value ratio	Higher LTV ratios are associated with increased risk.
2. Type of secured property	Single-family, detached units are the least risky; high-rise condominiums are the most risky.
3. Purpose of loan	If refinancing, those that remove equity are riskier than pure rate/term refinancings.
4. Lien status	Second mortgages are riskier than first mortgages.
5. Payment characteristics	Level-payment mortgage loans are less risky than increasing payment loans.
6. Geographic concentration	Increases in geographic concentration increase risk.
7. Seasoning	Seasoning decreases risk.
8. Pool size	Pools with fewer than 300 loans are considered riskier than pools with 300 or more.
9. Loan size	Loans greater than $300,000 are considered riskier than smaller loans.
10. Loan maturity	Faster amortization makes 15-year loans less risky than 30-year loans.

Source: Standard & Poor's Corporation, *S&P's Structured Finance Criteria,* 1988.

Most prepayemtn involves the repayment of mortgage loans in full before stated maturity. There are several reasons for such prepayment. Borrowers may choose to refinance their existing mortgages at lower rates. When prepayment occurs for this reason, investors tend to be on the short end of the stick because such refinancings occur in a falling interest rate environment. Thus, for a mortgage loan that carries an interest rate greater than the current market rate, the market value of the mortgage loan is greater than the face value, but a borrower can call his loan at face value.

Prepayment could also occur for such reasons as default and foreclosure, the sale of the property mortgaged, the payout of mortgage life insurance, or the full payout of hazard insurance following some disaster. Prepayments for these reasons do not necessarily imply an economic loss for investors. If they occur during a period of rising interest rates, investors could gain because the market value of the mortgage loan may be less than its face value.

The importance of prepayment risk to investors and issuers has been the impetus for new types of securities to eliminate prepayment risk. CMOs were developed to make the term of the securities more certain. CMO-holders are given a kind of "call protection," and this call protection is one of the primary reasons for the success of CMOs. CMO-holders can be reasonably certain that their bonds will not prepay (be called) prematurely. Because CMOs mitigate the prepayment risk, and provide shorter maturity classes of mortgage securities, investors who might not have otherwise invested in mortgages have been attracted to the mortgage securities market.

Concerns about prepayment risk have also encouraged many studies on the determinants of prepayment to be undertaken.[8] Such studies have found several important factors that

---

8 See, for example, Marcelle Arak and Laurie S. Goodman, "Prepayment Risk in Ginnie Mae Pools," *Secondary Mortgage Markets*, Spring 1985, and Helen F. Peters, Scott M. Pinkus, and David J. Askin, "Prepayment Patterns of Conventional Mortgages: Experience from the Freddie Mac Portfolio," *Secondary Mortgage Markets*, February 1984.

affect prepayment rates. In addition to some demographic factors, loan seasoning, interest rates, housing prices, assumability, and seasonality affect prepayment.

Seasoning refers to the age of the loan. In the first few years of mortgage loans, borrowers do not generally move and interest rates do not usually change enough to make refinancing profitable. The probability of prepayment, therefore, is low in the first few years of a mortgage loan and rises, although not steadily, thereafter.

Falling interest rates tend to increase prepayment rates (see Figure 3-12). In addition, to making refinancing attractive, falling interest rates also makes housing more affordable. Housing turnover and, therefore, prepayment rates tend to increase.

Assumability of a mortgage loan also tends to reduce prepayment rates, at least in a period of rising interest rates. FHA/VA loans are assumable, whereas conventional loans are not. FHA/VA loans and, therefore, GNMA pass-throughs tend to have lower prepayment rates than conventional loans and pass-throughs backed by conventional mortgage loans.

Interest-Rate Risk

Interest-rate risk is the third type of risk that is important for mortgage-backed securities. Interest-rate risk is the price sensitivity of an asset to changes in market interest rates. Interest-rate risk is usually measured by the duration of an asset. Duration is the average time to receipt of cash flows weighted by the present value of the cash flows. Duration is approximately equal to the percentage change in price for a given percentage change in market interest rates. In other words, it is the elasticity of price with respect to yield. The duration for a 30-year, fixed-rate mortgage loan with a 10-percent APR is 8.5 years if the loan is not prepaid. If market interest rates do not change and if the loan is prepaid in 15 years, the duration falls to 6.2 years. Thus, prepayment reduces interest-rate risk.

**Figure 3-12 Impact of Interest Rate Changes
on Prepayment Rates***

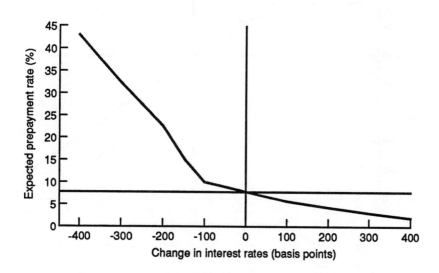

*For GNMA Pass-throughs with a 10 percent coupon issued at the end of
August 1987.
Source: Salomon Brothers.

Prepayment rates are low during periods of high interest
rates (when existing mortgage loans would be at a discount),
and they are high during periods of low interest rates (when
existing mortgage loans would be at a premium). So, for example, a 100-basis point increase in market rates does not have
the same impact as a similar interest-rate decrease (see Figure
3-13). Prepayments cause the market prices of mortgage loans
to rise more slowly than they fall. This is known as negative
convexity.

**Figure 3-13   Impact of Interest Rate Changes
on Price of Mortgage Securities***

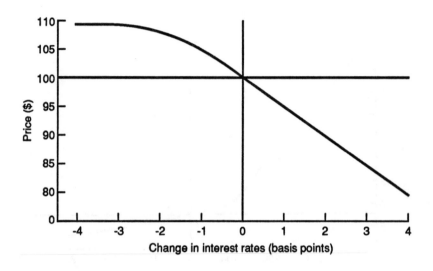

Change in interest rates (basis points)

---

*For GNMA Pass-throughs with a 10 percent coupon issued at the end of Ausgust 1987.

Source: Salomon Brothers

Returns

The most important components of the total risk of most mortgage-backed securities, therefore, are prepayment risk and interest-rate risk. For most mortgage securities—federal agency securities and their derivatives—credit risk is not important. To compensate investors for interest-rate and prepayment risk, federal agency pass-throughs have traded at 65 to 300 basis points above Treasury securities with comparable weighted average lives. Weighted average life (WAL) is the average time to the receipt of principal weighted by the principal payments. WAL rather than term to maturity is used to compare amortized assets with nonamortizing assets. The WAL of a Treasury security is equal to its maturity because all principal is paid at maturity. For amortizing assets such as a 30-year mortgage loan, the WAL is about 10 years, 20 less than the stated maturity. During 1986 and 1987, current-coupon GNMAs yielded about 200 basis points over comparable Treasuries. This spread reflects the falling interest rates of that period and, therefore, the likely negative effect of accelerated prepayments.

Future of Mortgage-Backed Securities

The market for mortgage-backed securities is nearing the completion of its second decade. Over 35 percent of all mortgage loans outstanding in 1987 were in the form of mortgage-backed securities. Less than six percent of auto loans were securitized in 1987 and less than four percent of credit card receivables were turned into securities.[9] For other types of assets the proportions are even smaller.

In addition, a secondary market for mortgage securities has developed, making such securities more liquid. Trading in mortgage-backed securities (mostly federal agency pass-throughs) increased from $230 billion in 1982 to more than $3 trillion in 1987 (see Figure 3-14). Turnover, as measured by the volume of trading in existing mortgage securities relative to the dollar amount of mortgage securities outstanding, has increased as well. In 1982, every dollar of mortgage securities outstanding was traded only 1.4 times annually. By 1987, it was traded nearly six times annually. Trading in mortgage securities, however, whether measured by volume or turnover, is still small compared to trading in Treasury securities.

The relevant issue regarding the future of the mortgage-backed securities market, therefore, is not whether the market will thrive, but rather what lies ahead for new securities backed by nonresidential mortgage loans and for new structures that make mortgage loans attractive investments to more investor groups.

---

9 These figures assume that the dollar amount securitized privately approximates the amount securitized publicly.

Figure 3-14   Trading in Existing Mortgage-Backed Securities

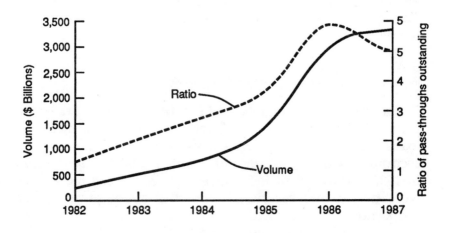

Source: Federal Home Loan Mortgage Corporation and the Board of Governors of the Federal Reserve System.

ARM-Backed Securities

While most mortgage-backed securities are backed by fixed-rate loans, securities backed by variable-rate and adjustable-rate loans have also been sold. Freddie Mac issued the first standardized ARM-backed security with ARMs that are tied to Treasury rates and have two percent annual caps and specified lifetime caps (usually six percent). In 1987, Fannie Mae introduced a standard ARM mortgage backed-security. Such standardization has greatly facilitated the growth and innovation of ARM-backed securities. Fannie Mae alone has issued over $20 billion in securities backed by adjustable-rate mortgages.[10]

10 Thomas A. Lawler, "Secondary Market Agencies Add Value to ARMs," *Savings Institutions*, January 1988.

And in 1988, Freddie Mac introduced a new mortgage-backed security backed by ARMs that carry the option to convert to fixed-rate loans.[11]

Commercial Mortgage-backed Securities

Commercial mortgage loans have been securitized along the lines of residential mortgage loans.

Salomon Brothers estimates that only three percent of the outstanding commmercial mortgage loans, including multifamily loans, had been securitized as of May 1987. Until December 1987, securities backed by commercial mortgage loans other than multifamily loans were collateralized by a single property and, therefore, were more akin to loan participations. One reason that most commercial mortgage-backed securities were collateralized by a single loan is that there is no standard commercial mortgage contract. Contracts vary not only by type of property mortgaged (e.g., office buildings, shopping centers, hotels), but contracts also vary within property groupings. Furthermore, the credit risk associated with commercial mortgage loans is very building- and market-specific, so that the evaluation of a pool of loans is difficult.

Although most commercial mortgage securities are not backed by a pool of loans, some commercial mortgage securities have been. In December 1987, Meritor Savings Bank formed a REMIC to pool $250 million in commercial mortgage loans. In March 1988, Chase Manhattan Bank received regulatory approval to set up a subsidiary to underwrite pools of commercial real estate loans, and in May 1988, a Boston-based mortgage company completed its first private placement of securities backed by a pool of small, fixed-rate commercial mortgage loans.

One type of commercial mortgage-backed security that is consistently backed by a pool of loans is the multifamily mortgage-backed security. Fannie Mae and Freddie Mac purchase multifamily mortgage loans and issue securities backed

11 Freddie Mac, *Annual Report*, 1987.

by them. In 1985, Freddie Mac issued the first mortgage-backed security backed exclusively by multifamily loans. In 1987, Fannie Mae developed the "delegated underwriting and servicing program," which permits mortgage lenders to sell mortgage loans to Fannie Mae without prior review. In exchange, the lenders share the losses with Fannie Mae. Owing to the success of this program, Fannie Mae was able to issue over $2 billion in multifamily mortgage-backed securities in 1987. By year-end 1987 $19 billion of mortgage securities backed by multifamily mortgage loans were outstanding.[12]

New Structures

In addition to the securitization of mortgage loans other than single-family loans, the second half of the 1980s has witnessed several new structures for mortgage loans. The impetus for new structures are twofold.[13] First, lower interest rates called attention to the prepayment option embodied in mortgage loans. Second, investors in mortgage securities became more sophisticated and better able to understand new structure, that would better manage prepayment risk.

In addition to REMICs, which have already been discussed and which are more reflective of a change in tax laws than a change in structure, several new structures of mortgage-backed securities have been developed. Most are variations on familiar themes.

One such variation is the stripped mortgage security, or simply "strip," which involves two classes of pass-through securities that receive different portions of principal and interest from the same pool of mortgage loans. For example, a pool of mortgage loans with an average APR of 10 percent might be stripped into a premium security with 14-percent coupon and a discount security with a six-percent coupon.

---

12 Federal Home Loan Mortgage Corporation.

13 Ann J. Dougherty, "Orchestrating New Securities," *Secondary Mortgage Markets*, Spring 1987.

The extreme version of a stripped security results in interest-only (I/O) and principal-only (P/O) securities. The interest-only classes receive primarily interest payments from an underlying pool of mortgage loans, while the principal-only class receives nearly all of the principal payments.

The origin of stripped securities is the early 1980s when the tax laws stimulated the development of Treasury strips.[14] Mortgage strips, however, first appeared in 1986, when such securities were privately placed and when Fannie Mae first offered strips publicly. During 1987, over $15 billion of strips had been issued.[15]

The success of strips stems from advantages to issuers as well as investors. Issuers of strips have been able to obtain larger total proceeds by stripping pass-through securities than by issuing only a single class of pass-throughs. Investors can obtain a premium mortgage security (I/O) with a low prepayment rate even during periods of falling interest rates; investors who want a discount mortgage security (P/O) with higher prepayment can find such securities even during periods of rising interest rates.

Both I/O and P/O strips can be valuable tools for hedging. I/Os can be used to hedge fixed-rate mortgage loans and other fixed income assets. As interest rates rise, the value of I/Os falls as does the value of other fixed-income assets. But prepayments will slow, generating greater than expected cash flows, which causes the value of I/Os to rise. If prepayments decrease enough, which they should do over most interest-rate scenarios, the value of I/O strips move inversely to the prices of other fixed-income assets.

P/O strips can also be used to hedge. They are used to hedge fixed-income liabilities rather than assets. As interest rates fall, the value of P/O stips increase because the rate at which the principal payments are discounted has fallen. This

14 See Sean Becketti, "The Role of Stripped Securities In Portfolio Management," *Economic Review*, Federal Reserve Bank of Kansas City, May 1988.

15 *Inside Mortgage Capital Markets*, Financial World Publications.

increase in value is reinforced by increases in prepayment. Thus, changes in the value of P/Os are inversely related to changes in the value of fixed-income liabilities as well as mortgage servicing fees, residual classes of CMOs and REMICs, and premium pass-through securities.[16]

Some Conclusions

The market for securities backed by residential mortgage loans is fairly-well developed and is clearly the most advanced market for asset-backed securities. Its success is largely attributable to the federal government for establishing the three federal agencies, which dominate the market for mortgage-backed securities, and for ultimately guaranteeing the mortgage securities of the federal mortgage agencies.

Most new developments in the market for mortgage-backed securities take the form of new types of securities. Other types of mortgage loans—commercial and multifamily—have been securitized and seem to show promise, but these types of mortgage securities have a long way to go to catch up with fixed-rate, residential mortgage-backed securities.

---

16 Dougherty, *Secondary Mortgage Markets*.

CHAPTER 4

Securities Backed by
▶ Auto Loans ◀

NEXT TO RESIDENTIAL MORTGAGE LOANS, automobile loans are the most securitized. During 1987, 63 percent of all non-mortgage asset-backed securities were collateralized by auto loans, and as of June 1988, more than $19 billion of auto loans had been securitized, representing seven percent of all auto loans outstanding.

This chapter examines asset-backed securities collateralized by automobile loans. The first section describes the underlying assets themselves—automobile loan contracts—and the second section examines the market for auto lending. The third section describes the characteristics of securities collateralized by auto loans. The fourth section examines the risks and returns of auto loan-backed securities. The fifth discusses the future of securities backed by auto loans.

Auto Loan Contracts

Automobile loans are made to individuals to finance the purchase of a car or light duty truck. They are generally level-pay, fixed-rate, self-amortizing loans that require monthly payments over a two- to five-year period. The actual life of an auto loan depends, however, on involuntary prepayment upon default and voluntary prepayments in the event of accelerated payment by the borrower or the sale or trade-in of the collateral.

Accrual Methods

Auto loans usually amortize according to one of three accrual methods—the actuarial method, the Rule-of-78 method, and the simple-interest method. The actuarial method is the same one used to calculate mortgage payments. The Rule-of-78 method is similar to the actuarial method in the derivation of the monthly payments; however, the proportion of each monthly payment that is devoted to paying down principal in the early months is greater under the actuarial method than under the Rule-of-78 method (see Table 4-1 and Figure 4-1).

Table 4-1   Payments under Different Accrual Methods: Actuarial vs. Rule-of-78

($5,000 loan with 60-month term to maturity
and 12 percent APR [monthly payment = $111.22])

Month	*Actuarial Method* Principal	*Actuarial Method* Interest	*Rule-of-78 Method* Principal	*Rule-of-78 Method* Interest
0	$ 0.00	$ 0.00	$ 0.00	$ 0.00
1	61.22	50.00	56.36	54.86
2	61.83	49.39	57.28	53.94
3	62.45	48.77	58.19	53.03
4	63.08	48.14	59.10	52.12
5	63.71	47.51	60.02	51.02
56	105.82	5.40	106.65	4.57
57	106.88	4.34	107.56	3.66
58	107.95	3.27	108.48	2.74
59	109.03	2.19	109.39	1.83
60	110.12	1.10	110.31	0.91
	$5,000	$1,673	$5,000	$1,673

**Figure 4-1   Principal Repayments as a Percent of
Monthly Payments: Actuarial vs. Rule-of-78s***

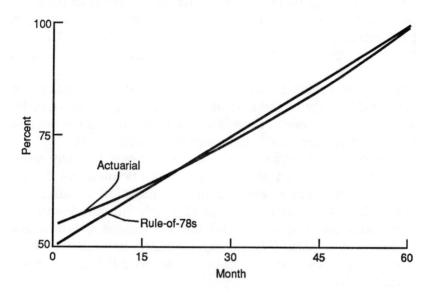

The reverse is true in the later months of the loan. The Rule-of-78 method, in effect, applies the sum-of-the-years-digits depreciation accounting principle to figuring monthly interest payments on a loan.[1] The reason that a creditor would use the Rule-of-78 method over the actuarial method is that it allows interest to be recognized earlier.

The actuarial and Rule-of-78 methods are methods of accrual that precompute interest, but the simple-interest method is not. Therefore, under the simple-interest method, the borrower receives the full benefit of accelerated payments and the full interest cost of late payments in addition to any late fees that might be assessed.

---

1 The amount of a monthly payment that is devoted to interest is $(N-t-1)/\Sigma\, t \times$ total interest paid over the life of the loan. N is the maturity of the loan in months and t is the current month. For example, the denominator of a one-year loan that makes monthly payments is $1 + 2 + \ldots + 12 = 78$, and the numerator for the first month is 12.

Table 4-2 compares the actuarial method of accrual and the simple-interest method. Under both methods, monthly payments would be the same. Under the actuarial method the portion of each monthly payment devoted to interest is precomputed according to an amortization schedule that assumes no prepayment. Under the simple-interest method, however, the portion of each monthly payment devoted to interest is not predetermined; it is based upon the outstanding principal balance of the loan at the beginning of each month. Accelerated payments, therefore, substantially reduce interest costs for borrowers under the simple-interest method.

Of course, if payments are late, a borrower will pay more interest under the simple-interest method. Some states do not allow late fees to be assessed until a payment is a certain number of days past due (e.g., 10 or 15 days). But simple-interest loans start accruing additional interest expenses, which are added to the outstanding principal balance, immediately. Late fees may be assessed on top of the additional interest when permitted by law.

The accrual method used is of no concern to the investor of securities backed by auto loans but is of concern to issuers because the accrual method used on underlying loans is important in structuring securities backed by auto loans. If a method other than the simple-interest method is used, accounting for the auto loans sold will have to be converted to the simple-interest method.

Terms

Auto loans are extended for both new and used cars. The terms for a new car loan differ slightly from those for a used car loan. For example, the average maturity of a loan for a new car is slightly under five years, while the average maturity of a loan for a used car is just under four years. As shown in Figure 4-2, the average maturity of loans on both new and used cars has been increasing since 1980. At that time, the average maturity of a new car loan was just under four years, and the average maturity of a used car loan was under three years.

Table 4-2 Payments Under Different Accrual Methods: Actuarial vs. Simple-Interest

($5,000 loans with 60-month term to maturity and 12 percent APR [monthly payment = $111.22])

| | Actuarial Method | | Simple-Interest Method | | | |
| | | | Payment Accelerated | | Late Payments | |
Month	Principal	Interest	Principal	Interest	Principal	Interest
0	$ 0.00	$ 0.00	$ 0.00	$ 0.00.	$ 0.00	$ 0.00
1	61.22	50.00	61.22	50.00	61.22	50.00
2	61.83	49.39	61.83	49.39	61.83	49.39
3	62.45	48.77	62.45	48.77	62.85	48.77
4	63.08	48.14	63.08	48.14	63.08	48.14
5	63.71	47.51	63.71	47.51	63.71	47.51
36	86.72	24.50	197.94	24.50	0.00	0.00
37	87.59	23.63	88.70	22.52	86.48	24.74
38	88.47	22.75	89.59	21.63	87.34	23.88
39	89.35	21.87	90.49	20.73	88.22	23.00
56	105.82	5.40	107.16	4.06	104.61	6.61
57	106.88	4.34	108.24	2.98	105.65	5.57
58	107.95	3.27	109.32	1.90	106.71	4.51
59	109.03	2.19	80.12	0.81	107.78	3.44
60	110.29	1.10	0.00	0.00	236.43	2.36
	$ 5,000	$ 1,673	$ 5,000	$ 1,644	$ 5,000	$ 1,677

Note: In the payment acceleration column, it is assumed that the borrower pays $222.44 instead of $111.22 in month 36. In the late payment column, it is asssumed that the borrower does not make a payment in month 36, and no late fee is ever assessed.

Figure 4-2   Average Maturity of Auto Loans Originated

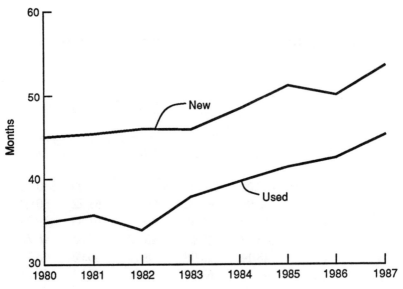

Source: Board of Governors of the Federal Reserve System.

The average annual percentage rate (APR) on a loan for a new car also differs from that for a used car (see Figure 4-3). The average APR on a new car loan has averaged 300 basis points above the two-year Treasury note rate, and the average APR on a used car loan has averaged 500 to 600 basis points above that. During periods of incentive-rate financing, the APR charged by the captive finance companies of the "Big Three" U.S. automobile manufacturers was far less than that charged by a commercial bank or credit union, often 50 basis points less and as much as 900 basis points less.

Finance companies as well as commercial banks extend automobile credit either directly to borrowers or indirectly through automobile dealers. Indirect loans are originated by dealers and then sold to the ultimate lenders. The ultimate lenders then may have recourse back to the dealer, although the trend has been moving away from recourse lending.

Figure 4-3   Average APR on a New Car Loan

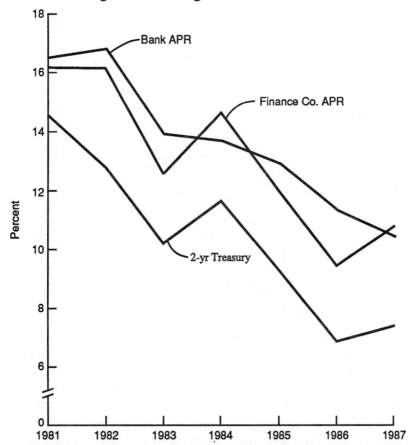

Source: Board of Governors of the Federal Reserve System.

The Market for Auto Lending

At year-end 1987, $261.4 billion of auto loans were outstanding, nearly three times the amount outstanding in 1978. As shown in Figure 4-4, auto lending has been growing faster than total consumer installment lending, particularly since 1981. At that time, auto loans represented 35 percent of total consumer installment loans outstanding, but by year-end 1987, auto loans accounted for nearly 43 percent.

Figure 4-4   The Growth of Auto Lending: 1978–1988

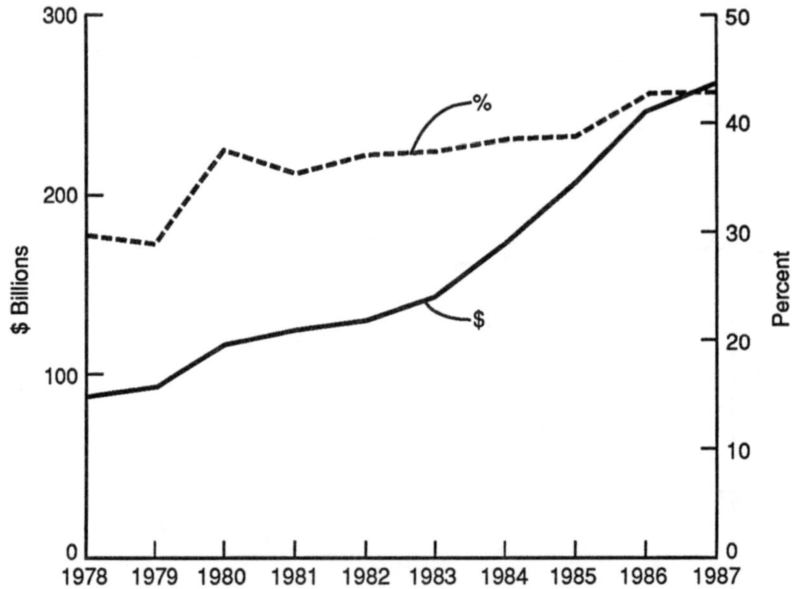

Source: Board of Governors of the Federal Reserve System.

Commercial banks have the largest share of the auto loan market, followed closely by finance companies (see Figure 4-5). Most of the finance company share is accounted for by the captive finance companies of the large U.S. automobile manufacturers—General Motors Acceptance Corporation, Ford Motor Credit Corporation, and Chrysler Finance Corporation. Since 1978, the captive auto finance companies have gained considerable market share from commercial banks. In 1978, finance companies accounted for less than 20 percent of all auto loans outstanding, but at year-end 1987, they commanded over 37 percent. Over the same time period, the market share of commercial banks fell from 60 percent to less than 41 percent.

Much of the increase in market share by the finance companies resulted from incentive-rate financing programs. The captive finance subsidiaries of the auto companies were originally formed to bolster the sales of their parents' products, especially when demand was weak and other lenders were decreasing their auto lending. Therefore, in periods such as 1981 and 1985-86, the captive finance companies of the U.S. automakers offered below-market-rate financing to boost the sale of their parents' products. During these periods, the auto captive finance companies increased their share of auto loans outstanding considerably.

Figure 4-5   Market Shares of Auto Loans Outstanding

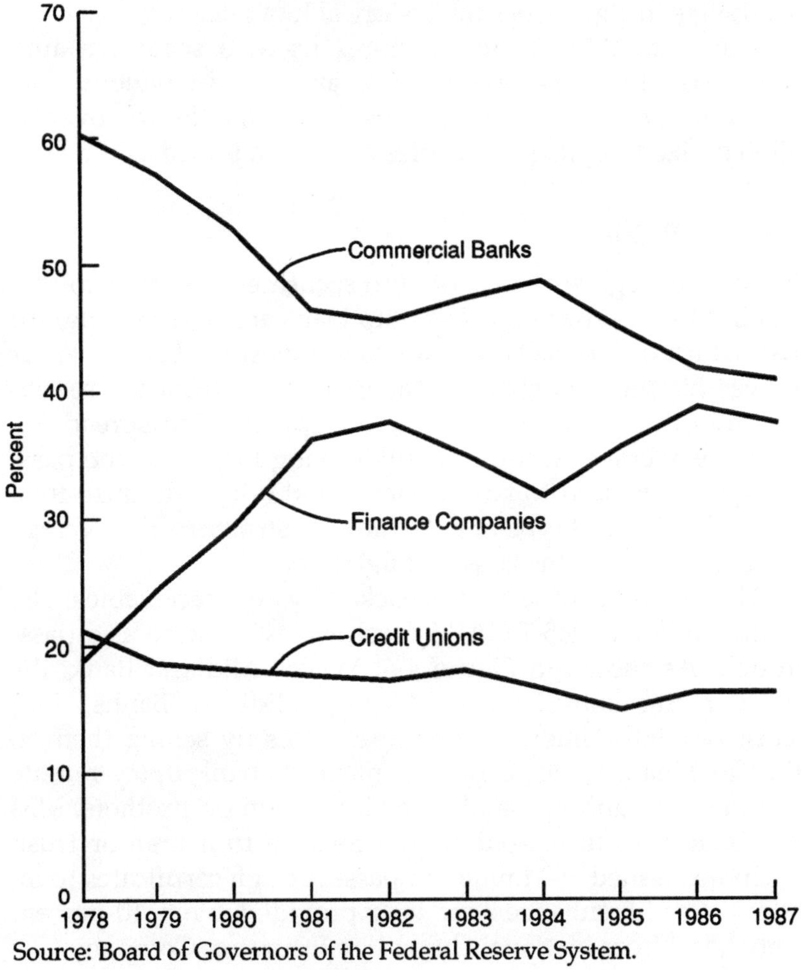

Source: Board of Governors of the Federal Reserve System.

Securities Backed by Auto Loans

Commercial banks, savings and loan associations, and finance companies have converted over $19 billion in auto loans to securities through public offerings, and it is estimated that an equal amount has been placed privately.

A typical security backed by auto loans pays principal and interest monthly and has a final maturity of three to five years. Most auto securities carry some form of credit enhancement, usually five to eight times the historical loss rate.

There are three basic structures used to securitize auto loans—pass-through, pay-through, and fixed-payment. The most common structure is the pass-through, although over $5 billion of fixed-payment securities have been issued.

Pass-Throughs

The pass-through structure of auto securities is similar to that of a GNMA pass-through. The auto loans are sold to a grantor trust, which in turn sells certificates to investors. Each investor receives his pro rata share of the cash flows from the receivables less the servicing and interest spread. The spread between the average APR on the underlying loans and the pass-through rate is used to pay servicing and other administrative fees. In the simplest type of pass-through structure, the average APR is greater than the pass-through rate.

The first issue of securities backed by auto receivables, The Marine Midland 1985-1 CARS Trust, was structured as a pass-through. As shown in Figure 4-6, Marine Midland Bank, the lead banking subsidiary of Marine Midland Banks, Inc., securitized $60 million of auto receivables by selling them to MM Car Finance, Inc., a limited purpose, bankruptcy-remote corporation established and owned by Salomon Brothers. MM Car Finance, in turn, sold the receivables to a grantor trust, which then issued $60 million of pass-through certificates to investors. Credit enhancement was provided by a 10-percent surety bond from National Union Fire Insurance Company.

Figure 4-6 MMCARS Finance Inc. (Structure)

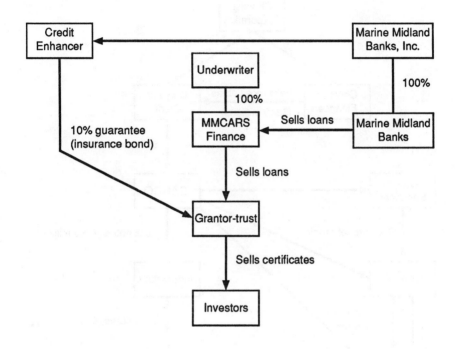

Pay-Throughs

An auto loan security structured as a single-class pay-through
bond is similar to a pass-through except that a limited-purpose
corporation is the issuer of debt. A multi-class pay-through is
similar to a CMO; a specified fraction of all cash received (less
servicing fees) is allocated first to pay interest and then to retire
principal. A pay-through bond is backed by the cash flows,
rather than the value of the collateral. To ensure that the cash
flows can support debt servicing, the issue is usually overcollateralized.

Figure 4-7   CARCO 86–1 (Structure)

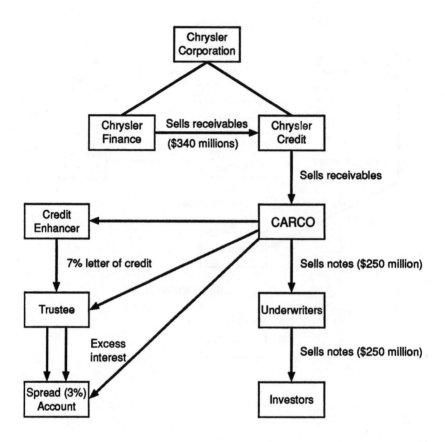

An example of an asset-backed security structured as a single-class pay-through is the CARCO 86-1 issuance of "Certificates of Automobile Receivables." In July 1986, Chrysler Finance Corporation, a wholly-owned subsidary of Chrysler Corporation, issued notes backed by automobile loans via Chrysler Credit Corporation, also a wholly-owned subsidiary of Chrysler, and Chrysler Auto Receivables Company (CARCO), a bankruptcy-remote, limited-purpose corporation.

As shown in Figure 4-7, Chrysler Finance sold auto loans valued at roughly $340 million to Chrysler Credit, which in turn sold them to CARCO. At that time, Chrysler Credit also injected a nominal amount of equity and a subordinated "advance" into CARCO, totalling roughly $91.25 million. CARCO issued notes, collateralized initially by a 75-percent participation interest in the portfolio of auto receivables, to investors for $250 million.[2]

Credit enhancement came from several sources. First, initial overcollateralization of two percent provided some credit protection. Second, CARCO set up a spread account with an initial value of $1.25 million and a maximum value not to exceed three percent of the outstanding principal on the auto loans. Third, CARCO purchased a seven-percent letter of credit from Union Bank of Switzerland. If funds available to pay monthly principal and interest to noteholders were insufficient, the deficiency was first made up from the funds in the spread account. If the funds in the spread account were insufficient, then the letter of credit was drawn upon. Subsequently, if excess funds were available after paying the noteholders and the servicing fee, the issuer of the letter of credit was reimbursed to the fullest extent possible.

Fixed-Payment

The third type of structure used to securitize auto loans is the fixed-payment structure. This structure assumes no prepayments. Payments (usually quarterly) to investors are fixed, i.e., they do not depend on the cash flows of the collateral. The fixed-payment structure is used most frequently for packaging incentive-rate loans; therefore, the interest rate paid to investors usually exceeds the average APR of the underlying loans, and between payment dates, funds are likely to be reinvested

---

2 Investors' notes were secured by a 75-percent participation until January 1, 1988, an 80-percent participation from January 1, 1988 through January 1, 1989, and a 90-percent participation thereafter.

at a rate higher than the average APR. Also, because payments to investors are fixed, prepayment is generally not an issue.

The fixed-payment structure was first used to securitize $4 billion of auto loans for General Motors Acceptance Corporation (GMAC). The underlying loans consisted of two pools of incentive-rate loans, with an overall average APR of 3.9 percent. As shown in Figure 4-8, GMAC sold the loans to Asset-Backed Securities Corporation (ABSC), a limited-purpose (orphan) subsidiary owned by First Boston. ABSC issued three classes of notes secured by $4 billion in auto receivables. ABSC then sold the receivables and the debt to an owner trust.

Interest to noteholders was fixed and paid quarterly. Since the underlying loans make monthly payments there was considerable reinvestment. This was performed by Morgan Guaranty, which issued a "guaranteed investment contract" of 5.807 percent. The notes were overcollateralized such that the cash flows from the underlying loans and any reinvestment income were sufficient to make payments on the notes.

Figure 4-8   ABSC–Series 1 (Structure)

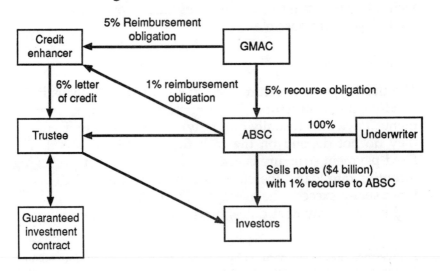

Principal was paid according to a schedule that assumes no prepayment. Principal of Class 1 noteholders was completely repaid before payment of principal to Class 2 noteholders was commenced, and principal of Class 2 noteholders was completely repaid before principal payments to Class 3 noteholders was commenced.

Credit enhancement was provided by GMAC's limited five-percent guarantee and by a six-percent letter of credit from Credit Suisse. If funds available to pay noteholders proved insufficient, the trustee could draw on the letter of credit up to the amount of GMAC's limited guarantee. Credit Suisse was then reimbursed by GMAC up to five percent. The letter of credit could also be drawn on if GMAC's limited guarantee were exhausted and the issuer failed to repurchase a limited amount (one percent) of certain defaulted receivables. The trustee, upon drawing on the letter of credit, would then be obligated to "pursue appropriate remedies against GMAC."

Risks and Returns

Regardless of structure, a security backed by a pool of auto loans involves some risks. Usually three types of risk—credit risk, interest rate risk, and prepayment risk—are important; however, prepayment risk is not relevant for fixed-payment structures. Of the three types of risk, credit risk is the primary concern of the rating agencies and credit enhancers.

Credit Risk

The five-year historical net loss and delinquency experience of an issuer is used as a first approximation of the expected loss rate of a pool of auto loans. As shown in Figure 4-9, the gross loss rate as well as the net loss rate on auto loans held by commercial banks has been increasing since 1983, and direct loans have higher loss rates than indirect loans. This is not because indirect loans are of greater credit quality than direct loans, but rather because some indirect loans have dealer recourse and, therefore, the dealer bears the credit losses. As shown in Figure 4-10, delinquencies are also higher now than they were in 1983, and delinquencies on indirect loans average 32 basis points more than those on direct loans.

In addition to the historical experience of the issuer's auto loan portfolio, eight other factors that have proven to significantly affect the loss rates of auto loan portfolios are used to estimate a pool's expected loss rate (see Table 4-3). These eight factors are 1) term-to-maturity, 2) seasoning, 3) loan-to-value ratio, 4) used vs. new car loans, 5) dealer recourse, 6) type of collateral, 7) geographic concentration, and 8) pool selection criteria.

Figure 4-9   Net Credit Loss on Auto Loans as a Percent of Auto Loans Outstanding

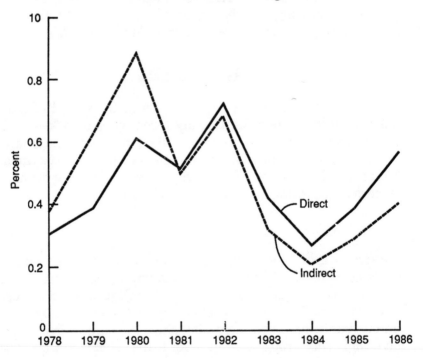

Source: American Banks Association.

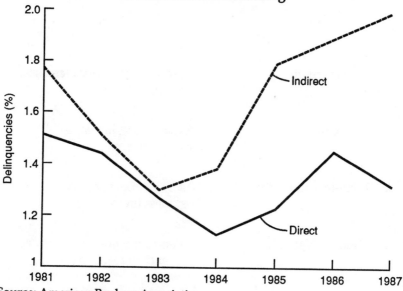

Figure 4-10   Auto Loan Delinquencies as a Percent of Auto Loans Outstanding

Source: American Bankers Association.

The first two factors concern the life of a loan. Term to maturity is the contractual life of a loan, and seasoning is the length of time that a borrower has been making loan payments. Seasoning, therefore, is concerned with the remaining life of a loan. Loans that have longer terms to maturity have slightly higher risk of delinquency than loans with shorter maturities. Loans that have more seasoning than others have lower default rates. Therefore, the riskiness of a loan with a long term to maturity diminishes as the length of time the borrower has been making payments increases.

The loan-to-value ratio of an auto loan is also a key determinant of that loan's expected loss rate. The loan-to-value (LTV) ratio is the loan amount as a fraction (or percentage) of the value of the collateral. For new cars, the value of the collateral is the amount of the dealer invoice, and for used cars, it is the National Automobile Dealer Association's "blue book" value. The LTV ratios for auto loans tend to be very high be-

Table 4-3 Factors that Affect the Riskiness of Auto Loan Pools

Factor	*Effect*
1. Term to maturity	As term to maturity increases, riskiness increases.
2. Seasoning	As seasoning increases, riskiness decreases.
3. Loan-to-value ratio	As LTV ratio increases, riskiness increases.
4. Used vs. New car	Loans to finance used cars are riskier than loans to finance new cars.
5. Type of automobile	Certain autos may be riskier than other (e.g., lesser quality or defective).
6. Recourse vs. nonrecourse	Loans with dealer recourse are not as risky as loans without it.
7. Geographic concentration	As geographic concentration in auto loan pool increases, riskiness increases.
8. Pool selection criteria	Other than modified random sample, may be riskier.

Source: Duff & Phelps Inc. and Standard & Poor's.

cause lenders often extend credit to finance the entire purchase price of a car. The average LTV ratio for a loan for a new car is between 90 and 95 percent, and the average LTV ratio for a used car loan is between 95 and 99 percent. As shown in Figure 4-11, the average LTV ratios have been increasing for both new and used car loans.

Loans with high LTV ratios tend to be more risky than loans with low LTVs primarily for two reasons. First, high LTVs imply that the borrower has a very small equity interest in the collateral. Second, should the borrower default, there is a greater possibility of less than full recovery on high LTV loans from the sale of a repossessed vehicle.

Figure 4-11   Average Loan-to-Value Ratios for Auto Loans

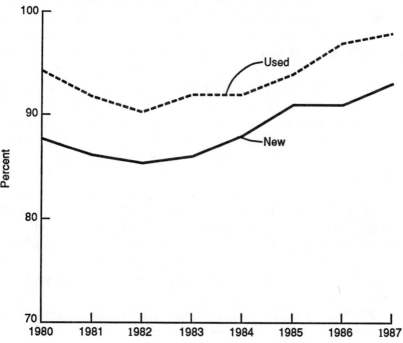

Source: Board of Governors of the Federal Reserve System.

Two other determinants of expected loss have to do with the type of collateral. Loans to finance the purchase of used cars are more risky than loans to finance the purchase of new ones. In fact, the loss severity and the cumulative net losses can be two to three times greater for used car loans than for new car loans.[3] In addition, sometimes auto loans for the purchase of cars that appeal to a select group (e.g., high-priced sports cars or vary low-priced economy cars) and, therefore, have a limited resale market, and loans for cars of known lesser quality or with known major defects are riskier.

As alluded to before, indirect loans that carry dealer recourse are less likely to have credit losses than loans with no recourse. Again, this is because the credit losses are borne by the dealer and not by the creditor.

Another key factor in assessing the expected loss rate of a pool of auto loans is the geographic concentration of the pool. If loans are highly concentrated in a few geographic areas, especially economically depressed areas, the expected loss rate would be adjusted upward. Pools of auto loans that were originated by one bank or savings and loan association are more likely to be highly concentrated geographically than pools originated by the auto finance companies because the finance companies have a nationwide network, while banks and S&Ls tend to do most of their auto lending in one state or one region.

The last key determinant of expected losses is the pool selection criteria. The most common is the "modified random sample" basis. A random sample is chosen from an issuer's entire portflio after excluding loans with less than six months of seasoning and delinquent loans. If these exclusions are not made, the expected loss rate on the pool would be adjusted upward.

As mentioned previously, these risk factors are more of a concern to the credit enhancers and rating agencies than to investors. This is because credit enhancement usually protects

---

3 "Rating of Auto Receivables," Duff & Phelps, Inc.

the investor against losses that would be five times greater theexpected default rate. There are, however, two other types of risk that securities backed by auto loans entail—prepayment risk and interest rate risk—that are of concern to investors.

Prepayment Risk

Prepayment risk is not a big component of the overall riskiness of a security backed by auto loans. The cash flows of securities backed by auto loans are certain if a fixed-payment structure is used, and they are very stable for pass-throughs and pay-throughs. Auto loan borrowers rarely refinance because the APRs on used car loans are much greater than the APRs on new car loans. Also, the short maturities of auto loans make principal a large component of each monthly payment; therefore, even major changes in prepayments have a minor effect on the weighted average life (WAL) and yield of auto loans.

WAL is the average time to receipt of principal weighted by the amount of each principal payment. WAL, rather than term to maturity, is used to compare amortizing assets with nonamortizing assets. The WAL of a Treasury security is equal to its term to maturity, but the WAL of an auto loan, depending on prepayments, is usually between two and 2.5 years for a 60-month loan; therefore, in such an auto loan should be compared with a two- or 2.5-year Treasury security.

As shown in Figure 4-12, prepayment rate of an auto loan has very little influence on the WAL of a portfolio of auto loans. In the case of a portfolio of 60-month loans with 12-percent APRs, the WAL with no prepayment would be 33.5 months. If the prepayment rate were a constant 20 percent, the WAL would be just under 30 months.

Few factors are known to affect the prepayment rates of auto loans.[4] First, prepayment increases with seasoning. Second, loans for used cars pay off faster than loans for new cars, especially in the early months of a loan. Third, loans with

---

4 Salomon Brothers.

**Figure 4-12   Impact of Prepayments on WAL and Duration
($5,000, 60-months, APR=12%)**

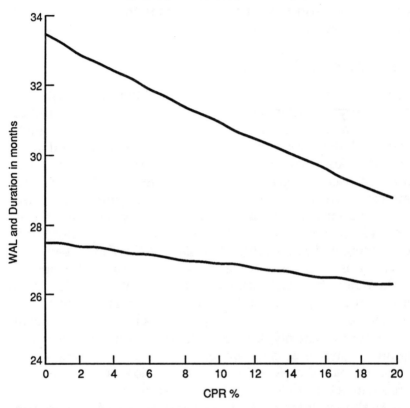

high APRs pay off faster than loans with relatively low APRs; therefore, incentive-rate loans are generally expected to have very low prepayment rates. Fourth, short-term loans (36-months) pay off faster than long-term loans (48- or 60-months).

Interest-Rate Risk

The third component of the riskiness of a security backed by auto loans is interest-rate risk—the sensitivity of the price of an asset to changes in market interest rates. Duration is the measure usually used to analyze interest-rate sensitivity. Duration is the average time to receipt of cash flows weighted by the present value of the cash flows. Duration is approximately equal to the percentage change in a security's price divided by the percentage change in interest rates; i.e., it is the price elasticity with respect to interest rates. The greater an asset's duration, the more sensitive it is to changes in interest rates. As shown in Figure 4-12, the duration of an auto loan with a 60-month term to maturity is between 26 and 27.5 months, depending on the rate of prepayment. This means that for reasonably small changes in interest rates (less than 50 basis points), the market price of such an auto loan contract changes by less than five percent (see Figure 4-13). Even a 100-basis-point change in interest rates would translate into less than a 10-percent change in the market price of such an auto loan.

**Figure 4-13   Impact of Interest Rate Movements
on the Price of Auto Loans**

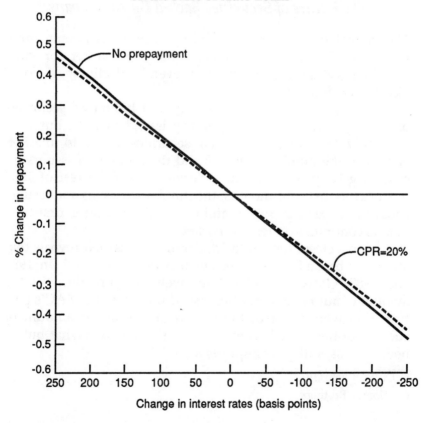

Returns

Securities backed by auto loans "have consistently offered substantial yield premiums relative to comparable corporate debt."[5] For example, in September 1987, GMAC medium-term notes with a WAL of 1.5 years yielded about 20 basis points less than GMAC auto loan-backed securities with a WAL of 1.5 years.[6]

Securities backed by auto loans also have been priced at considerable premiums relative to comparable Treasury securities. Since 1985, the yield on auto loan-backed securities has averaged 75 basis points above Treasury securities with comparable maturities (see Figure 4-14).

The Future of Securities Backed By Auto Loans

The market for securities backed by auto loans is only three years old. While it may appear that the market for such securities has leveled off and may even be declining, a closer look indicates otherwise.

As shown in Table 4-4, nearly $10 billion of securities backed by auto loans were publicly issued in 1986, but 1987 saw only $6.4 billion of such securities come to market. However, the number of issues and the number of issuers increased greatly over that time period, and if the rest of 1988 mirrors the first four months, the number of issues and issuers should be greater in 1988 than in 1987. Furthermore, first-time issuers continue to enter the market.

Even a closer look at the dollar amount issued reveals that securities backed by auto receivables show promise. In 1986 and 1987, GMAC accounted for well over one-third of the amount of auto loan securities issued publicly. If GMAC's participation were ignored, the growth in the dollar amount of such securities issued seems to have slowed somewhat but is, nevertheless, still quite impressive.

---

5 Duff & Phelps Inc.

6 Salomon Brothers.

Figure 4-14 Average Spread over Treasuries for Securities Backed by Auto Loans (WAL Less than 2 Years)

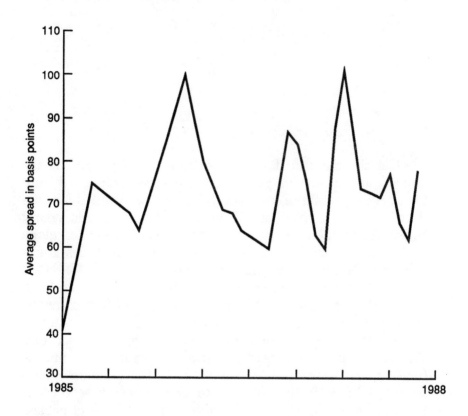

Source: *Asset Sales Report,* various issues.

Table 4-4   History of the Public Market for Securities
Backed by Auto Loans

Year	Number of Issues	Number of Issuers	Number of New Issuers	$ Amount Issued ($Millions)
1985	5	5	5	$898.6
1986	14	7	5	9,660.6
1987	21	11	6	6,363.8
1988 (June)	10	8	2	2,253.5

Source: *Asset Sales Report*, various issues.

Clearly, the auto finance companies, and GMAC as the largest, are important players in the securitization of auto loans. All auto finance companies combined accounted for one-third of the auto-loan-backed security issues sold and nearly two-thirds of the dollar amount issued in 1987. GMAC alone accounted for nearly one-quarter of the auto securities issues sold and 37 percent of the dollar amount issued.

While there is a premium to be paid for issuing auto loan-backed securities, rather than medium-term notes or commercial paper, there are also some benefits, which are likely to encourage the finance companies to continue to issue securities backed by auto loans. Such securities provide an additional funding source for the finance companies. The duration of auto securities is perfectly matched to that of the assets being funded. In addition, funding auto loans with asset-backed securities often does not require the addition of debt or equity to the balance sheet. This benefit is expected to become more important because, as of December 1988, the financial statements of majority-owned subsidiaries must be consolidated with those of their parents.[7]

These benefits of securitization also apply to commercial banks, the largest collective auto lender, and to S&Ls. For these depository institutions, however, the ability to fund a portfolio

---

7 See Chapter 7 for a more detailed discussion on consolidation of subsidiaries.

of loans without raising additional equity may be the greatest benefit of securitization because banks and thrifts are required by regulation to hold a certain proportion of equity capital against every dollar of assets on their balance sheets and because of the tax laws, equity is a more expensive funding source than debt. Proposed guidelines for risk-based capital for banks are unlikely to reduce the proportion of capital required to be held for consumer loans; therefore, the economizing on capital is likely to continue to be a key advantage of securitization of banks and thrifts.

The benefits to sellers of securities backed by auto loans seem strong enough to ensure the continued issuance of these securities. Institutional investors, in effect, can invest in a low-risk pool of auto loans priced at a considerable premium over comparable U.S. government securities, without having to acquire a distribution network or expertise in originating and servicing the loans.

CHAPTER 5

Securities
Backed by
▶ Credit Cards ◀

THE FIRST SECURITIES BACKED BY CREDIT CARD RECEIVABLES were sold in March 1986. The issue was a $50-million private placement by Salomon Brothers for Bank One of Columbus, Ohio. As of June 1988, nearly $5 billion of securities had been publicly offered. Credit card-backed securities account for about one-third of nonmortgage asset-backed securities that have been publicly offered since 1987, but they represent only about 3.5 percent of credit card debt outstanding.

This chapter discusses securities backed by credit card receivables. The first section describes credit card accounts and credit card debt. The second section discusses the market for credit cards. The third section discusses the securities backed by credit cards and analyzes the various structures used to securitize credit card receivables. The fourth section examines the risks and returns of such securities, and the final section discusses the future of securities backed by credit cards.

Credit Card Accounts

A credit card account is an unsecured revolving line of credit supported by the customer's contractual obligation to pay. The cardholder can draw on the line of credit to make purchases from a participating merchant or, in some instances, to borrow money through a cash advance.

Types of Credit Cards

In general, there are two types of credit cards—general purpose cards and proprietary cards. Bank cards and travel and entertainment (T&E) cards are general-purpose; that is, they can be used to make purchases wherever the cards are accepted. Retail and oil company cards are proprietary; usually, they can be used only at outlets of the issuer. General purpose cards account for only 29 percent of all cards, yet they account for over 70 percent of all credit card debt. Proprietary cards account for over 70 percent of all cards, but less than 30 percent of all credit card debt (see Figure 5-1).

Oil company cards and T&E cards, such as the American Express green card, Diners Club, and Carte Blanche, are not true "credit" cards. These card plans do not generally allow cardholders to pay off their balances over an extended period of time. Consequently, their ratios of volume to outstandings are much higher than they are for bank cards or retail cards (see Figure 5-2). Oil company cards and T&E cards also generate a relatively small dollar amount of outstandings compared with other types of cards. Furthermore, the maturity of debt generated by these cards is usually less than 60 days. Oil company card and T&E card debt, therefore, are not likely candidates for securitization.

Bank cards and retail cards are true "credit" cards. They allow cardholders to extend payments on outstanding balances over time. Usually there is a 30-day grace period in which no interest is charged. For cash advances on bank cards, however, finance charges usually start accruing from the time the funds are borrowed.

Figure 5-1   General Purpose versus Proprietary Cards

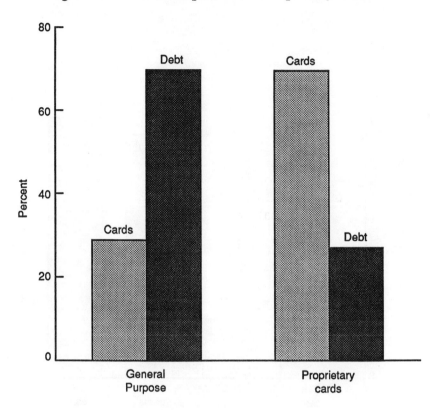

Source: *The Nilson Report*, September 1986, No. 338 and the Board of Governors of the Federal Reserve System.

Retail Cards

Retail Cards are two-party arrangements that involve an issuer—a retailer—and a cardholder. The retailer issues a card and establishes a line of credit for the cardholder. The cardholder can then draw against that line of credit by making purchases at the retail outlets of the issuer. Typically, retail cards carry low credit limits and have less demanding credit qualification requirements.

Figure 5-2 Ratio of Volume to Outstandings

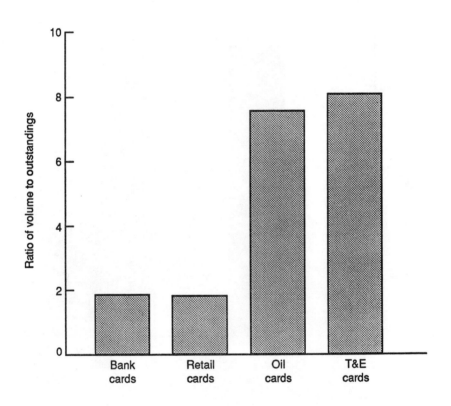

Source: *The Nilson Report*, March 1988, No. 424.

Table 5-1 lists the top five retail credit card issuers in the United States. Sears is by far the largest issuer of retail cards with over 27 million active accounts, $14.2 billion in charge volume, and $14.1 billion in outstandings. J.C. Penney ranks second, with Montgomery Ward, Federated Department Stores, and May Department Stores coming in third, fourth, and fifth.

Table 5-1 Top Five Issuers of Retail Credit Cards

	Active Accounts (Millions)	Charge Volume ($Billions)	Debt Outstanding ($Billions)
Sears, Roebuck & Co.	27.3	$14.2	$14.1
J.C. Penney Co.	18.2	7.3	4.2
Montgomery Ward & Co.	9.0	3.7	3.5
Federated Dept. Stores	9.8	4.0	1.5
May Department Stores	9.0	4.1	1.6
Percent of Total	53.1%	51.3%	58.6%

Source: *The Nilson Report*, November 1987, No. 439.

Retail cards can be run in-house or through private-label companies. Private-label companies may simply administer the credit card accounts, or they may also extend the credit. As shown in Table 5-2, the top five private label companies that provide both administrative services and credit (ranked according to outstanding credit card balances) were GE Capital, Citicorp, Household Retail Services, First Data Resources, and Total System Services. General Electric Credit, in 1988, managed 14 million active accounts, and Citicorp managed 3.3 million active accounts.

Table 5-2 Top Five Issuers of Private Label Retail Credit Cards

	Active Accounts (Millions)	Charge Volume ($Billions)	Debt Outstanding ($Billions)
GE Capital Corp.	14.0	$ 7.6	$ 7.1
Citicorp Retail Services	3.3	1.4	1.1
Household Retail Services	0.8	0.8	0.8
First Data Resources	1.9	1.0	0.7
Total System Services	0.6	1.0	0.7

Source: *The Nilson Report*, No. 441, December 1988.

Bank Cards

Bank cards, such as Visa and MasterCard, are three-party arrangements. They involve the issuer—usually a bank but sometimes a savings and loan association or a credit union—the cardholder, and the merchant. Unlike most issuers of retail cards, the issuer of a bank card has no affiliation with the cardholder nor with the merchant involved in a transaction.

In exchange for the line of credit, some banks charge an annual fee, but all banks charge interest on outstanding credit card balances. Annual fees range from zero to $20 for standard cards and from zero to $45 for premium cards. The average annual percentage rate (APR) on credit card debt is 18 percent and ranges from 12.5 percent to 21 percent. Often interest does not accrue, however, if the outstanding balance is paid in full within 30 days of the billing date. A cardholder who pays his balance in full each month is called a convenience user. According to Visa, about one-third of monthly billings require no finance charges.

A cardholder receives a bank card from an "issuing" or "participating" bank. An issuing bank sets up its own card operation. It obtains a license to use the Visa or MasterCard logo; determines the nature and price of services offered to the cardholder; establishes a credit limit; sets annual fees, interest rates, and payment and finance charge calculation procedures; arranges for or handles the processing of credit card sales slips; and holds the receivables generated by its credit card accounts. A participating bank is a bank that offers its customers the bank card of an issuing bank. Participating banks may or may not choose to hold the receivables generated by its customers' credit card accounts.

The largest credit card issuers are issuing banks. Consequently, only issuing banks are likely candidates to securitize credit card debt. As shown in Table 5-3, the top 10 issuers of bank cards account for 32 percent of all active accounts, 32 percent of charge volume, and 38 percent of total bank card debt outstanding. The largest bank card issuer is Citibank with 6.8

million active Visa and MasterCard accounts, $11.8 billion in charge volume, and $9.2 billion in outstandings.

Table 5-3   Top Ten Issuers of Bank Credit Cards

	Active Accounts (Millions)	Charge Volume ($Billions)	Debt Outstanding ($Billions)
Citibank, Sioux Falls	6.8	$11.8	$9.2
Bank of America	4.9	8.0	5.3
Chase Manhattan, Wilmington	3.5	5.7	4.5
First Chicago	3.4	5.5	3.8
Manufacturers Hanover	2.3	3.8	2.5
Chemical Bank	1.6	2.4	1.3
Maryland National Bank	1.5	3.0	2.0
Wells Fargo	1.3	2.1	2.1
Marine Midland	1.2	2.0	1.2
Associates National, California	1.0	1.1	1.0
Percent of total	32.1%	31.7%	38.2%

Source: *The Nilson Report*, No. 406, June 1987.

As shown in Tables 5-4 and 5-5, the largest bank card issuers among credit unions and savings and loan associations are dwarfed by the commercial banks. Citibank has about 45 times as many active accounts, 64 times as much charge volume, and 103 times the receivables as the Texas Credit Union League, the largest issuer of bank cards among credit unions. Similarly, Citibank has 12.5 times the active accounts, nearly eight times the charge volume, and 18 times the outstandings of USA Federal Savings, the largest issuer of bank cards among S&Ls.

Table 5-4 Top Five Issuers of Bank Credit Cards Among Credit Unions

	Active Accounts (Thousands)	Charge Volume ($Millions)	Debt Outstanding ($Millions)
Texas Credit Union League	150	$185	$89
Navy Federal Credit Union	95	180	135
Dearborn Federal Credit Union	47	70	23
Pentagon Federal Credit Union	41	81	40
State Employees Credit Union	34	31	19

Source: *The Nilson Report,* No. 415, November 1987.

Table 5-5 Top Five Issuers of Bank Credit Cards Among Savings and Loan Associations

	Active Accounts (Thousands)	Charge Volume ($Millions)	Debt Outstanding ($Millions)
USAA Federal Savings, San Antonio	540	$1,550	$502
Atlantic Financial Federal, Philadelphia	363	500	434
Western Savings of Arizona	258	364	249
Chevy Chase Federal Savings, Maryland	256	499	260
Imperial Savings, San Diego	167	375	167

Source: *The Nilson Report,* No. 414, October 1987.

The Market for Credit Cards

At year-end 1987, $146 billion in revolving consumer debt was outstanding. Credit card receivables represent the largest share of such debt. As shown in Figure 5-3, credit card debt has been growing faster than total consumer installment debt. In 1978, credit card debt was less than 18 percent of total consumer debt outstanding, but by 1987, it was nearly 24 percent.

Figure 5-3   Growth of Credit Card Debt*

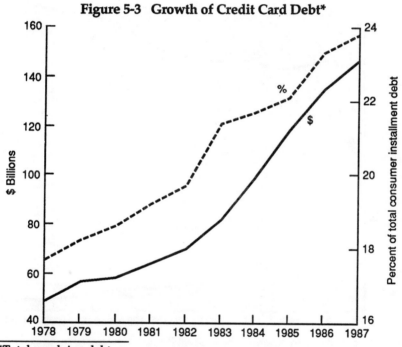

*Total revolving debt
Source: Board of Governors of the Federal Reserve System.

There are four primary issuers of credit cards—commercial banks, retailers, oil companies, and thrift institutions (savings and loan associations, savings banks and credit unions). As shown in Figure 5-4, market shares of credit card debt have changed considerably since 1978. At that time, commercial banks accounted for 50 percent; retailers, 43 percent; and oil companies, nearly seven percent. In 1987, commercial banks accounted for 65 percent of total credit card debt outstanding; retailers, nearly 25 percent; oil companies, two percent; and thrift institutions, six percent.

Figure 5-4   Market Shares of Total Revolving Credit

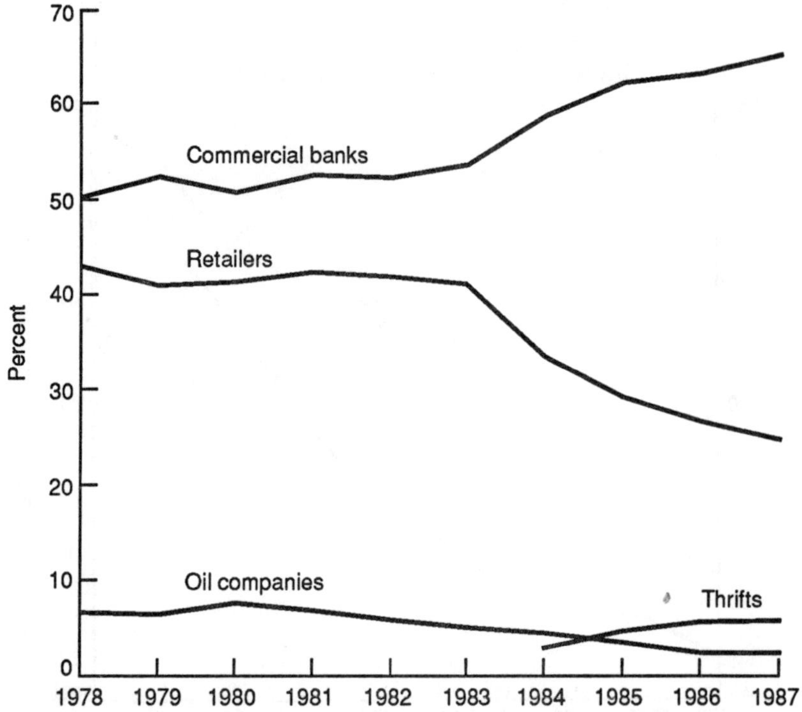

Source: Board of Governors of the Federal Reserve System.

The use of bank cards as a payment vehicle and as a major source of unsecured credit began to take off in the late 1970s. From 1976 to 1979, the number of bank card accounts rose 65 percent to 75 million, and the number of transactions rose 62 percent to 1.3 billion (see Figure 5-5). Credit card debt outstanding at banks more than doubled over this time period.

Figure 5-5 Growth of Bank Card Usage
(Millions)

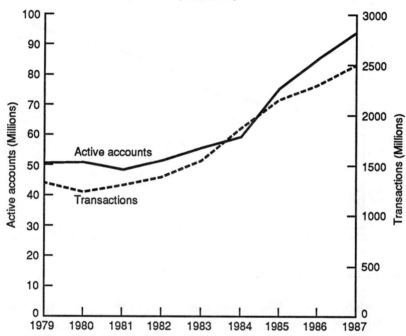

Source: *The Nilson Report,* various issues.

Just as bank card programs were showing promise, however, soaring interest rates made usury ceilings binding, bringing the growth in bank cards to a halt. In addition, the credit restraint measures of 1980 reduced the use of bank cards. These setbacks, however, were only temporary. The special credit restraints, initiated in March 1980, were phased out beginning in July of the same year. Usury ceilings became less binding, either because they were relaxed or because credit card operations shifted to states that did not have usury ceilings. Since 1981, the growth of bank card activity has been strong, particulary over the 1983-84 period when the number of bank card transactions grew 34 percent. During 1984, bank cards were used for 4.3 percent of all consumer spending, compared to 3.6 percent in 1983 (see Figure 5-6).

Figure 5-6   Percent of Consumer Spending on Bank Credit Cards

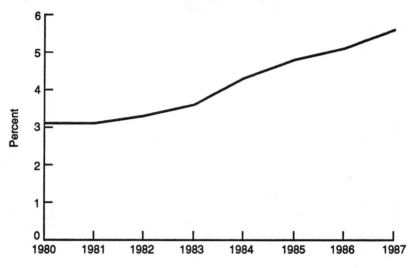

Source: *The Nilson Report*, No. 424, March 1988.

Also, during 1984, banks made a big push to expand their credit card operations by mass mailing pre-approved credit card applications. As shown in Figure 5-7, credit card debt as a percentage of total consumer installment debt at banks increased since 1978; the biggest gains have taken place since 1984. Around that time, retailers increasingly accepted bank cards alongside their proprietary cards. Consequently, retailers started losing market share to banks.

Credit Card Securities

The first securities backed by credit card debt were issued by commercial banks and savings and loan associations and were collateralized by bank card (Visa and MasterCard) receivables. Relative to mortgage-backed securities or securities backed by auto loans, few issues of credit-card-backed securities have come to market. Consequently, their structures are much less standardized. Nevertheless, as with other asset-backed securities, credit card securities are structured either as collateralized debt or as participation interests in a pool of assets.[1]

Figure 5-7   Total Revolving Credit at Commerical Banks

Source: Board of Governors of the Federal Reserve System.

Some Common Features

Whether an issue is structured as debt or as participations, all credit card securities have some characteristics in common. All credit card securities have some type of overcollateralization, stipulate interest-only periods, provide for payout events, and allow for cleanup calls. These characteristics are necessary because of the nature of credit card accounts (see Table 5-6).

---

1 Issues structured as collateralized debt have included commercial paper backed by credit card receivables.

Table 5-6   Common Features of Credit Card-Backed Securities

Feature	Comments
Overcollateralization	Claim to cash flows from all collateral pledged or claim on fixed dollar amount of a portfolio.
Interest-only period	For the first 18 months or more of a credit card-backed security's life only interest is paid on outstanding principal balance of securities.
Payout event	Premature termination of interest-only period.
Cleanup call	Retirement of securities when principal balance reaches a certain percentage of original amount.

Source: Standard & Poor's and Moody's Investor Service.

Unlike residential mortgage loans and automobile loans, credit card loans are not self-amortizing assets. Most credit card issuers require a minimum monthly payment—usually a percentage of outstanding balances (typically five percent) or a minimum dollar amount, whichever is greater. Cardholders, however, have the option to pay any amount above the minimum, and payment terms vary among lenders. Payment rates, therefore, vary significantly. The average monthly payment rate was 14 percent in 1987.[2]

---

2 VISA.

Historically, credit card balances have been paid down quite rapidly. The expected life of a credit card portfolio is only six to eight months.[3] Therefore, to extend the life of securities backed by credit cards, such securities stipulate an interest-only period, during which time only interest is paid on the outstanding principal balance of the securities. Any principal payments made during that time are, in effect, reinvested in the new charge volume and additional receivables generated by the same group of accounts that serve as collateral for the securities.

Outstanding balances from a portfolio of credit card accounts can also vary significantly. The reason is twofold. First, payment rates vary. Second, cardholders have the option to draw on their lines of credit up to their limits as they choose.

Outstanding balances vary significantly, and investors do not want to see the value of the outstanding credit card accounts fall below the outstanding principal balance on the securities. Therefore, the dollar amount of receivables sold to a limited-purpose finance company or to a trust to back an issue of credit card securities exceeds the dollar amount of the securities issued. When credit card backed securities are structured as the debt of the issuer, the securities are overcollateralized; the investors are given a claim to the cash flows from all of the receivables pledged as collateral.

When credit card-backed securities are structured as interests in a portfolio of receivables, two classes of securities are issued—an investors' class and a seller's class. The investors' class represents a participation interest in a portfolio of credit card accounts, which during the interest-only period, is a fixed dollar amount equal to the face value of the certificates issued, rather than as a percentage of the portfolio of credit card receivables. Therefore, as the balance of credit card receivables falls, the investors' participation rises and as the balance of credit card receivables rises, the investors' participation falls, in

3 Standard & Poor's, *S&P's Structured Finance Criteria*, 1988.

percentage terms. During the interest-only period, the seller's interest is the residual interest in the underlying portfolio.

A payout event—also called an "amortization event" or a "liquidation event"—allows for the premature termination of the interest-only period. Payout events can be "viewed as safety valves which allow the deal to wind down early if certain potentially adverse events occur."[4] Events that trigger payout include a substantial decline in yield on the portfolio of credit card accounts, a significant increase in losses or delinquencies on the portfolio, a significant change in cardholder payment or borrowing habits that adversely affects the portfolio, or default on the part of the issuer, servicer, or the trustee.

In addition to the payout event, which can reduce the life of securities backed by credit cards, most credit card-backed securities also include a "cleanup call." This allows the issuer to retire the securities when the principal balance reaches a certain percentage of the original amount (e.g., two percent).

Credit Card-Backed Notes

The first issue of credit card securities, a $50 million private placement for Bank One, was structured as participations in a pool of assets. The first public offering of securities backed by credit card receivables, however, was structured as collateralized debt rather than participations. It was a $200-million issue of 7.15-percent notes by RepublicBank Delaware in January 1987. The structure of the issue is shown in Figure 5-8.

The collateral for the issue was a $240-million portfolio of credit card accounts that had an average APR of 16.9 percent. The bulk of the credit card accounts were purchased by RepublicBank Delaware from RepublicBank Dallas, rather than originated by the Delaware bank. Both banks are subsidiaries

---

4 Standard & Poor's.

of RepublicBank Corporation. The accounts not purchased from the Dallas bank were originated by the Delaware bank.

RepublicBank Delaware issued notes for $200 million and pledged the $240-million portfolio to the trustee as collateral. The notes, therefore, were overcollateralized by roughly 20 percent at the time the notes were issued. Further credit enhancement was provided by a $10-million letter of credit and a reserve fund, or a spread account.[5] The reserve fund had a required balance equal to five to seven percent of the outstanding balance on the notes.

Figure 5-8   RepublicBank, Delaware, Credit Card-Backed Notes (Structure)

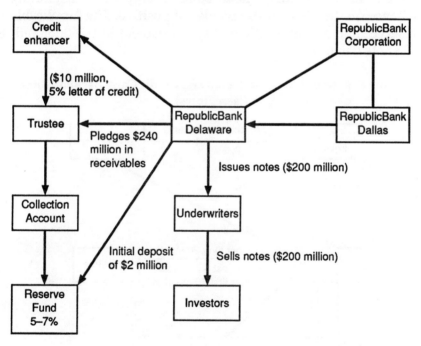

---

5 The mechanics of spread accounts are detailed in Chapter 2.

The cash flows of the RepublicBank issue are shown in Figure 5-9. Cardholders make interest and/or principal payments on their credit card balances to RepublicBank Delaware. During the interest-only period, RepublicBank then transfers funds to the collection account up to the amount necessary to make the collection account balance equal the "required collection account balance" plus the amount necessary for the current reserve fund balance to equal the "applicable reserve fund amount" plus any amount necessary to reimburse the issuer of the letter of credit for drawings on the letter of credit. The "required collection account balance" is the interest due and payable on the notes on the next payment date plus difference between the outstanding note balance and the outstanding balance on the pledged receivables, if positive. The "applicable reserve fund amount" is five to seven percent of the outstanding note balance.

**Figure 5-9   RepublicBank, Delaware, Credit Card-Backed Notes
(Cash Flows)**

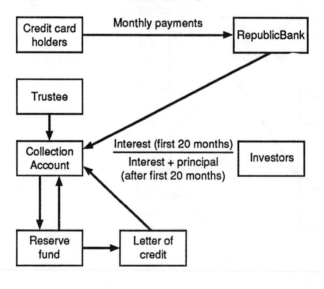

During the period when principal and interest are paid, RepublicBank Delaware transfers all collections on the pledged receivables to the collection account. On each payment date during this period, interest is paid on the notes and principal payments are also made. Principal payments will equal the amount held in the collection account after transfers necessary to the reserve fund and to the letter of credit are made, or the minimum principal payment, whichever is greater. The minimum principal payment is the amount by which the outstanding balance on notes exceed the outstanding balance on the pledged receivables.

Credit Card-Backed Certificates

As of June 1988, the largest issue of securities backed by credit card receivables was the $800-million First Chicago CARDS Trust. As shown in Figure 5-10, FCC National Bank and First National Bank of Chicago, both subsidiaries of First Chicago Corporation, sold $1.3 billion in credit card receivables to a trust. The trust then issued $800 million in certificates backed by the portfolio of credit card accounts. The certificates represented the investors' interests in the $1.3-billion portfolio. Their interests were fixed at $800 million for the first 18 months (the interest-only period), and thereafter decreased by the principal payments made and any charge-offs borne by the investors. The residual value of the portfolio represented the seller's interest. Charge-offs were allocated proportionately to the investors' interests and to the seller's interests, but a letter of credit covered the investors' share up to $136 million.

The cash flows for this issue are shown in Figure 5-11. During the interest-only period, credit card holders make monthly payments to First Chicago. These payments consist of finance charges and principal. The principal component is reinvested in new receivables generated by the set of accounts in the trust. The proportion of finance charges allocated to the investors' interests in the receivables are transferred to a collection account, and the trustee then pays the certificate-holders their share of monthly interest, the servicer his servicing fees, and the issuer of the letter of credit any reimbursements due.[6] Remaining finance charge income is paid to the sellers. If funds in the collection account are insufficient to pay the certificate-holders, the trustee draws on the letter of credit. During the amortization period, cardholders make payments to First Chicago, and First Chicago passing along the investors' share of principal and interest to investors via the collection account and the trustee.

Figure 5-10   First Chicago CARDS Trust 1987–1

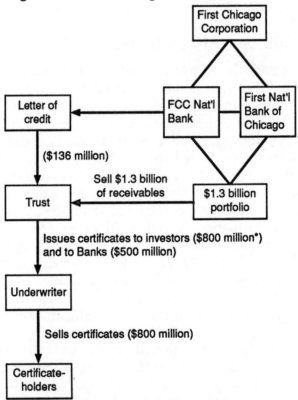

*Certificateholders interest in portfolio is fixed at $800 million for first 18 months.

---

6 Also, any amounts drawn under the letter of credit, the repurchase price for any receivables repurchased by the sellers, and any investment income from amounts previously in the collection account are transferred to the collection account.

Figure 5-11   First Chicago CARDS Trust 1987-1
(Cash Flows)

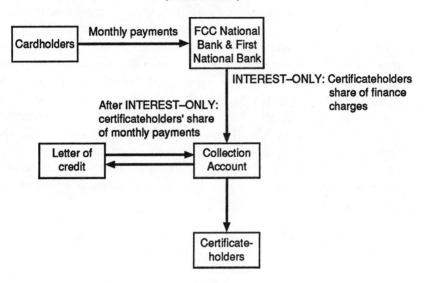

Risks and Returns

Securities backed by credit card accounts are not risk-free. Investors face credit risk, interest-rate risk, and repayment risk. Because of the short maturity of credit card securities, interest-rate risk and repayment risk are not major components of the overall riskiness of credit card-backed securities. The primary concern, at least of the rating agencies and the credit enhancers is credit risk.

Credit Risk

As with mortgage-backed and auto loan-backed securities, the rating agencies use the historical loss and delinquency experience of an issuer's portfolio of loans (from which the pool for securitization is selected) as a first approximation of the expected loss rate on the securitized pool of receivables. As shown in Figure 5-12, net losses and delinquencies on credit card balances have been rising since 1983, despite a favorable economic environment. The likely culprit in the deterioration of the overall credit quality of credit card portfolios is the increase in the proportion of accounts acquired through mass mailings of pre-approved cards and the increase in poor quality credits at banks that have aggressively attempted to increase their share of the bank card market.

Figure 5-13 shows how credit card loss and delinquency experience compares with that of auto loans. Since 1978, the ratio of credit card net losses to those from direct auto loans has ranged form 2.8 to 6.6. In recent years, net losses on credit card receivables have been more than six times as great as net losses on auto loans.

Figure 5-12   Credit Card Losses, Delinquencies and Unemployment

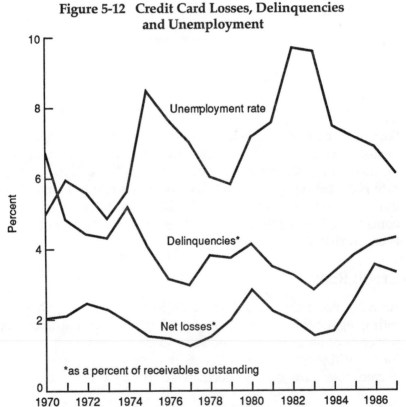

Source: *The Nilson Report*, various issues, The Board of Governors of the Federal Reserve System.

Figure 5-13   Ratio of Bank Card Net Losses to Net Losses from Auto Loans

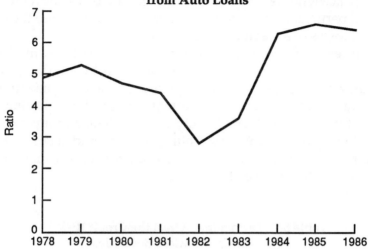

Sources: American Bankers Association and *The Nilson Report.*

In addition to historical loss and delinquencies, other factors also play an important role in the performance of credit card portfolios. The rating agencies have identified six key factors that affect the riskiness of a credit card portfolio.[7] These factors are listed in Table 5-7.

Geographic and demographic concentration will likely increase the risk of a credit card portfolio, particularly if it has a high concentration of accounts in parts of the country or with groups of people known to be more affected by economic downturns.[8] Geographic regions that have been experiencing unstable growth and that are dependent upon a small number of industries are affected more by economic shocks; therefore, a portfolio with a high proportion of credit card accounts drawn

---

7   Moody's Investors Service, "Credit Card Receivables: Moody's Examines the Risk, " *Structured Finance Research & Commentary,* July 1987 and *S&P's Structured Finance Criteria.*

8   Moody's Investors Service.

from such regions would be riskier. Similarly, a high proportion of accounts of low-income individuals or of individuals from a particular profession or industry would increase the expected losses of a credit card portfolio.

In recent years, credit card issuers have instituted marketing plans that attempt to attract new accounts by offering cards to "affinity groups." In such plans, various organizations cooperate with a bank to help promote its card by appealing to the potential cardholders' loyalty to a particular group or association. Affinity group marketing plans would increase the concentration of certain cardholder characteristics, which may increase the risk of a portfolio.

Table 5-7 Factors that Affect the Credit Risk
of Credit Card-Backed Securities

Factor	Comments
1. Geographic concentration	Increases in geographic concentration increase risk.
2. Demographic concentration	Increases in demographic concentration increase risk.
3. Seasoning	As seasoning increases, risk decreases.
4. Method of acquisition	Pre-approved mass mailings generate riskier accounts.
5. Underwriting criteria	Widespread use of "scoring system overrides" increases risk.
6. Pool selection criteria	Accounts should be at least one year old and not more than 30 days delinquent.

In addition to its effect on concentration, method of acquisition is a factor that affects portfolio performance because of its implications for credit risk of individual accounts. Issuers usually solicit credit card accounts in two ways—pre-approved mailings and "take-one" applications. Take-one applications are usually displayed in bank lobbies and in outlets of participating merchants. Accounts generated through mass mailings tend to be riskier than accounts that are approved after a more rigorous credit evaluation than is possible with pre-approved accounts. But, if credit card applications are not evaluated thoroughly and properly, an account generated from such an application can be expected to perform no better than one generated from a pre-approved application.

Credit scoring models are often used to evaluate credit card applications. When such models are used, the accuracy of the models and the way in which they are used are crucial to the loss experience of the accounts that the models generate. Widespread use of "scoring system overrides," where a credit officer overrides the recommendation of the scoring model, will likely increase the loss rate of a credit card portfolio.[9]

Another important factor that affects the performance of a portfolio of credit card accounts is seasoning, or the age of an account. The older the account, the less risky it is. Seasoning allows cardholders to establish a track record, and allows the issuer to weed out weaker accounts.

Pool selection criteria will also significantly affect the expected loss rate for a pool of accounts. According to Standard & Poor's, each account in a pool for securitization should be at least 12 months old, not be 30 days or more delinquent, have a billing address in the United States, have a credit limit under $10,000, not be that of an employee of the issuer, and not be restricted by the issuer as to its use.[10]

---

9 Moody's Investors Service.

10 Standard & Poor's. Many pools have accounts with credit limits that exceed $10,000, but these account for a very small proportion of entire pool.

One other factor affects credit risk. This factor is the servicer. The experience of the servicer as well as the manner in which the servicer works out delinquent accounts affect the riskiness of an issuer. For example, some servicers in working out delinquent accounts re-age them—reclassify them as nondelinquent. Such practices may mask credit risk by making historical experience unreliable for assessing the credit risk of a pool of accounts.

The rating agencies use historical performance as well as the factors discussed above to assess the level of credit enhancement necessary for the rating desired by the issuer. Portfolio performance varies greatly from issuer to issuer; therefore, the level of credit enhancement necessary also varies. Public deals have had letters of credit that cover five to 35 percent of the principal balance on the securities issued, and many deals include forms of credit enhancement in addition to letters of credit, such as overcollateralization, and spread accounts. Therefore, with credit enhancement equal to several times the historical default rates of credit card portfolios, credit risk is less of a concern of investors than of the rating agencies and credit enhancers, although investors will experience losses if the credit enhancement proves insufficient.

Repayment and Interest-Rate Risk

Investors are not protected against repayment risk and interest-rate risk. Because of the short maturity of credit card-backed securities and structures that consist of lengthy interest-only periods, however, these risks are relatively small.

Because there are no scheduled payments on credit card debt beyond the required minimum, an increase in the repayment rate (rather than the prepayment rate) poses risks to investors of credit card-backed securities. Repayment rates are highly cyclical, with repayments slowing in the fourth quarter because of the holiday season. As shown in Figure 5-14, however, the repayment rate on credit card portfolios has been falling in recent years. This may be attributable to the addition

Figure 5-14 Credit Card Repayment Rates

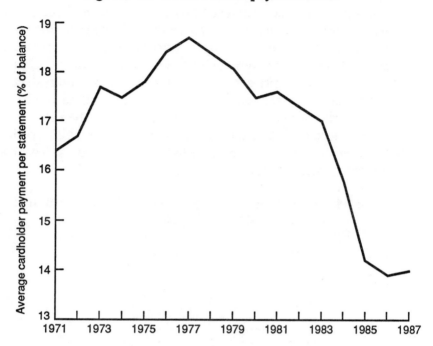

Source: VISA.

of less seasoned accounts and to increased reliance by consumers on revolving credit.

Since 1972, the average monthly repayment rate has
ranged from 12 to 18 percent. At 12 percent, the weighted
average life (WAL) of a credit card-backed security would be
two years, and at 18 percent it would be 1.8 years (see Table
5-8). WAL is the average time to receipt of principal weighted
by the amount of each principal payment, which equals the
time when half of the principal can be expected to have been
repaid. Similarly, a jump in the repayment rate from 12 to 18
percent would decrease the duration of the security by only 2.5
months. Repayment rates, therefore, affect the WAL and duration (and hence the price and yield) of a credit card-backed
security very little.

Duration approximates the elasticity of price with respect to changes in market interest rates. As shown in Table 5-8, a one percent change in interest rates would change the price of a credit card-backed security by between 1.8 and 2.3 percent, depending on the repayment rate. Figure 5-15 plots the percentage change in price that would result from interest rate swings. Interest rates would have to move more than 100 basis points for the price to increase or decrease more than two percent. Furthermore, after consideration of the probability of interest rate movements, the expected change in the price of a credit card-backed security is only 0.10 percent.

Table 5-8   Effect of Repayment Rates on WAL and Duration of Credit Card-Backed Securities*

Repayment Rate	WAL (years)	Duration (years)
8%	2.5	2.3
10	2.3	2.1
12	2.2	2.1
14	2.1	2.0
16	2.0	1.9
18	2.0	1.8

* Assumes a 7.8 percent coupon, 18-month interest-only period, and stated final muturity of 60 months.

Source: Michael Waldman and Thomas Delehanty, "Introduction to Credit Card-Backed Securities," Salomon Brothers, August 1986.

Returns

In addition to the WAL, duration, and yield of a credit card-backed security, repayment rates can also affect the net yield of a credit card portfolio. An increase in repayment rates reduces the balance of credit card receivables on which finance charges

Figure 5-15 Impact of Interest Rate Movements on Price of Credit Card-Backed Securities*

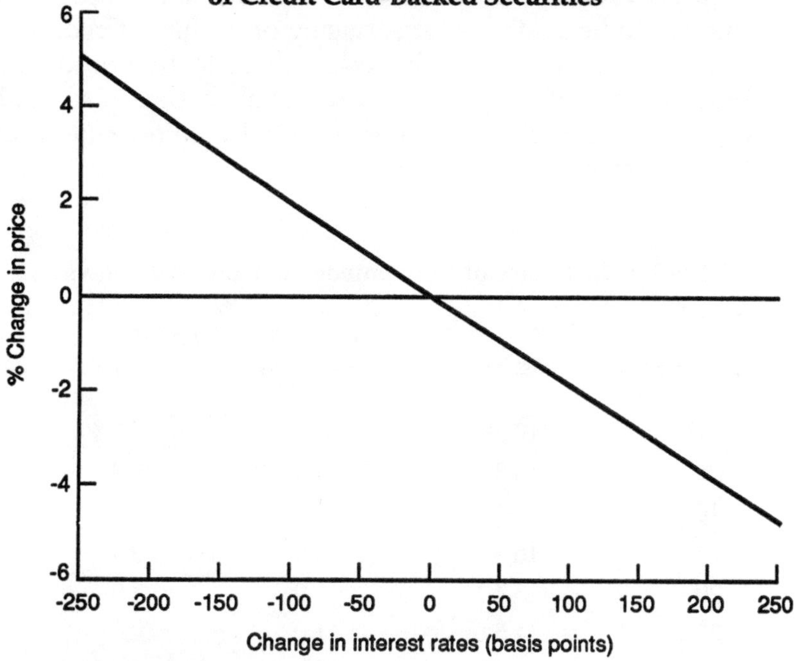

Change in interest rates (basis points)

*Assumes a constant 12 percent repayment rate.

Source: Salomon Brothers.

are calculated and, therefore, reduces the gross yield of the portfolio. According to the Federal Reserve System's 1986 Functional Cost Analysis Survey, the average gross yield on credit card portfolios is 14.3 percent and the proportion of active accounts that paid finance charges was 74 percent. If that 74 percent is assumed to be the proportion of nonconvenience users, the average APR on credit card accounts is 19.3 percent.

Table 5-9 illustrates the effect of the spread between the gross yield on a credit card portfolio and the rate on securities backed by such a portfolio (assumed to be nine percent). At the current average convenience use rate of 25 percent, the spread between the gross yield and the rate to investors would be 550 basis points. However, 350 basis points can be expected to be consumed by charge offs, leaving 200 basis points for servicing and cushion. If convenience use were to increase to 35 percent, nothing would be available for servicing or cushion. Credit enhancement, however, generally covers three to five times the historical charge-off rate; therefore, convenience use and charge-offs could increase quite substantially before investors would be affected.

Table 5-9   Influence of Convenience Use on Cash Flows

Convenience Use	Gross Yield	Less (3.5%) Charge-offs	Less 9% Pass-Through Rate
0%	19.3%	15.8%	6.8%
5	18.3	14.8	5.8
10	17.4	13.9	4.9
15	16.4	12.9	3.9
20	15.4	11.9	2.9
25	14.5	11.0	2.0
30	13.5	10.0	1.0
35	12.5	9.0	0.0

Securities backed by credit card receivables have been priced at about 80 basis points above comparable Treasury securities (see Figure 5-16). This spread reflects investors' perceptions of the riskiness and lack of liquidity relative to comparable Treasuries.

The Future of Credit Card-Backed Securities

Securities backed by credit card receivables are a relatively new product, and therefore their future success is difficult to determine. The first issue of securities backed by credit card receivables was not sold until 1986, and no public offerings of such securities were sold until early 1987.

**Figure 5-16 Yield on Credit Card-Backed Securities
Spread over Treasuries**

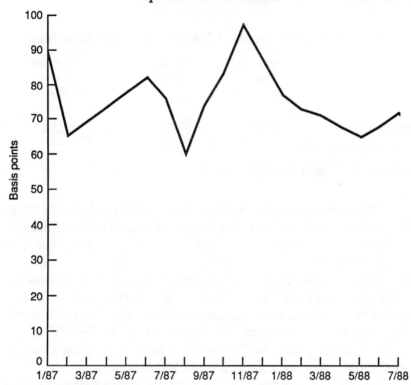

Source: *Asset Sales Report,* various issues.

In their first full year of existence, $2.4 billion of credit card-backed securities were issued publicly. This $2.4 billion consisted of seven issues by six different issuers. The largest issuer was First Chicago, with a single $800-million issue, followed by Bank of America, with two issues for a total of $700 million.

In the first six months of 1988, six issues of credit card-backed securities, totalling $2.5 billion were sold publicly (see Table 5-10). The largest of these three was a $600-million issue by First Chicago, a $500-million issue of Maryland National Bank, the seventh largest issuer of bank cards, and a $500-million of Sears, Roebuck and Company, the largest issuer of retail credit cards.

Table 5-10   Public Issues of Credit Card-Backed Securities

	Number of Issues	Number of Issuers	$ Amount Issued ($ Billions)
During 1987	7	6	$2.4
Through June 1988	6	6	2.5

Source: *Asset Sales Report*, various issues.

First Chicago's $600-million issue was its second for 1988. Earlier that year, the banking firm had issued $300-million in certificates backed by credit cards through a master trust. The master trust, pioneered by First Chicago, represents a major innovation in credit card securitization. A master trust allows the issuer to make continuous offerings of securities with minimal additional work. A master trust, therefore, signifies the issuer's intention to sell these types of securities repeatedly. Within the first two-months of establishing the master trust, First Chicago used it twice to issue credit card-backed securities.

In addition to Sears, J. C. Penney, the second largest issuer of retail cards, and Montgomery Ward & Company, the third largest issuer, filed with the SEC to issue credit card-backed securities. J.C. Penney will issue between $200 and $300 million in securities through a master trust. Wards filed to sell $240 million in credit card securities.

The entrance of the retailers to the asset-backed market should be a boost of credit card-backed securities. Sears, Penney, and Ward hold nearly 15 percent of all credit card debt and, therefore, are expected to be important players in the asset-backed market. The retailers, however, are not expected to dominate the market as issuers because the number of banks with sizable bank card operations is quite large relative to the retailers.

CHAPTER 6

▶ More Than Homes, ◀ Cars, and Plastic

RESIDENTIAL MORTGAGE LOANS, automobile loans, and credit card receivables, while the most frequently securitized assets, are not the only securitized assets. Many others have been pooled, packaged, and sold as securities. Most of these assets are installment loans or similar to installment loans. Others carry a government guarantee. Yet, there are several types of assets that have been securitized that are not similar to installment loans, nor are they guaranteed by the U.S. government. This chapter discusses the securitization of installment-type loans other than auto loans and credit card receivables, government-guaranteed and government-related loans, and certain types of commercial loans.

Installment Loans

Assets that have reasonably predictable cash flows and are easily understood are ripe for securitization. As discussed in the preceeding chapters, residential mortgage loans, auto-

automobile loans, and credit card receivables fit this description. But the list does not end there. This section discusses the securitization of other intallment-type loans, including leases, loans for manufactured housing, and other consumer debt.

Leases

Lease receivables were the first type of nonmortgage asset to be securitized. In May 1985, Comdisco, the largest independent lessor of computer equipment, privately issued $35 million of 4 1/2-year notes backed by computer leases. Since then, other computer leases as well as leases for automobiles and medical equipment have been securitized (Table 6-1).

A lease is a contract by which one conveys real estate, equipment, or facilities for a specified term for a specified rent. The owner of the leased asset is known as the lessor; the user of the asset is the lessee.

There are two types of leases—finance leases and operating leases. Only finance leases have been securitized. Finance leases, also known as capital and full-payout leases, extend over most of the leased asset's useful life. An operating lease is a short-term lease that the lessee has the option to cancel. Finance leases either cannot be canceled or are cancelable if the lessee reimburses the lessor for any losses that are incurred as a result of cancellation. When a finance lease is terminated, either the leased asset reverts to the lessor or the lessee may purchase the asset.

Like loans, financial leases are a source of financing. The cash flows from a lease are similar to those from an installment loan. That is, payments are usually level. They are the amortized value of the asset less its residual value. Payments under a finance lease contract, in effect, comprise principal and interest, much the same way that installments on an auto loan consist of principal and interest.

The primary differences between a loan and a lease concern ownership and bankruptcy status. Ownership of an asset financed with a loan resides with the user of the asset; ownership of an asset financed with a lease resides with the lessor, not the lessee, the user. As the owner of the asset, the lessor receives the tax benefits. These benefits have diminished somewhat since passage of the Tax Reform Act of 1986.

Table 6-1   Securitization of Lease Receivables (Selected Issues)

Date	Issuer	Collateral	Amount	Type of Security
3/85	Sperry	Computer leases	$192.5	Notes
9/85	Sperry	Computer leases	145.8	Notes
12/86	Sperry	Computer leases	174.5	Notes
12/86	Goldome FSB	Computer leases	205.7	Notes
3/87	Volvo*	Auto leases	232.7	Notes
8/87	Volkswagen	Auto leases	150.0	Notes
10/87	Scientific Leasing*	Medical equipment leases	19.5	Notes
10/87	American Airlines	Notes to finance leases for aircraft	92.6	Pass-throughs
12/87	Volvo*	Auto leases	149.3	Notes
3/88	Scientific Leasing*	Medical equipment leases	9.6	Notes

*Private placements.

Sources: *Asset Sales Report*, various issues.

Lessors and lenders have different rights under the bankruptcy laws, which tend to make financing an asset with a lease rather than a loan a riskier venture for the financier. If a lessee defaults on a lease, the lessor can recover the asset, but if the asset is worth less than the present value of future lease payments, the lessor can try to recoup the difference in bankruptcy court. The lessor's claim, however, is limited to one year's lease payment for a bankrupt firm and three years' lease payments for a reorganized firm.

In contrast, if a borrower defaults on a loan, the lender has prior claim on the loan's collateral. If the value of the collateral is less than the present value of the unpaid principal and interest, the lender can enter a claim for the full difference.

There are three basic types of lessors—bank-related, captives, and independents. Bank-related lessors are either commercial banks or subsidiaries of bank holding companies. Captive lessors are subsidiaries of manufacturers. They lease their parents' products. Bank-related lessors have dominated the market for finance leases over the last two decades.[1] Nevertheless, independents and captives have dominated the securitization of lease receivables.

As of June 1988, only six public issues of securities backed by lease receivables, valued at nearly $1 billion, had been sold. Sperry Corporation, a manufacturer of computer equipment, issued over $500 million of lease-backed notes through three separate issues in 1985 and 1986.[2] A grantor trust established by Goldome FSB, a federally-chartered mutual savings bank, issued over $200 million in notes backed by computer leases in 1986. In 1987, VW Credit, a subsidiary of the German auto manufacturer Volkswagen AG, issued $150 million in auto lease-backed notes through a special-purpose corporation. Also, in 1987, American Airlines issued $93 million in pass-

---

1 U.S. Department of Commerce, *U.S. Industrial Outlook*, 1988.
2 Sperry and Borroughs Corporation merged in 1986 to form Unisys.

through certificates backed by notes to finance leases for aircraft.

In addition to the lease-backed securities issued publicly, at least $500 million of such securities had been sold privately by June 1988. Such private placements have included securities backed by leases for automobiles, computers, and medical equipment.

The structures of securities backed by leases are similar to those backed by auto loans and credit card debt. As shown in Figures 6-1 to 6-3, Sperry's issues of lease-backed securities were essentially pay-through notes, while Goldome's issued pass-through certificates. Volkswagen issued asset-backed notes with interest paid semi-annually and principal payable upon maturity.

Figure 6-1   Sperry Lease Finance Corporation
(Structure)

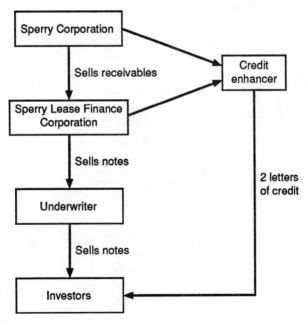

Source: The First Boston Corporation.

Figure 6-2   Goldome 1986–A Grantor-Trust (Structure)

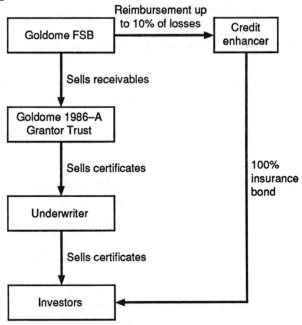

Source: The First Boston Corporation.

Figure 6-3   Volkswagen Lease Finance Corporation (Structure)

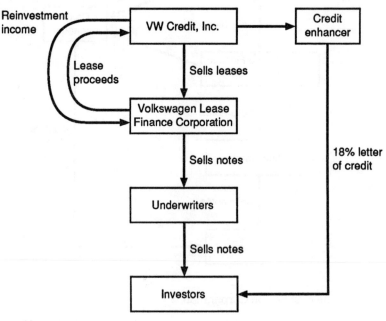

Source: The First Boston Corporation.

Loans for Manufactured Homes

Loans for manufactured homes are another type of consumer installment debt that have been securitized along the same lines as residential mortgage loans and auto loans.[3]

Loans for manufactured homes are usually considered loans for personal property rather than for real estate. The borrowers generally earn lower incomes than do home owners. Also, manufactured homes usually depreciate, rather than appreciate in value. Consequently, the loan-to-value ratio on loans to finance the purchase of either type of home may rise rather than fall as the loan matures. Rates on manufactured home loans, therefore, are usually 200 to 400 basis points higher than mortgage rates. Most manufactured home loans usually have maturities of 10 to 15 years.

Like mortgage loans, loans for manufactured homes are either FHA/VA loans or conventional loans. The guarantee on VA manufactured home loans is essentially a 100-percent guarantee. The guarantee on FHA manufactured home loans, however, is not as comprehensive. The FHA guarantees 90 percent of each loan, but does not reimburse a lender more than 10 percent of the loans it produces annually. Thus, an FHA lender that has $10 million in manufactured home loans outstanding can receive a maximum of $1 million from the FHA, even if $5 million of loans default.

Loans for manufactured homes are generally indirect, nonrecourse loans. That is, manufactured home dealers originate the paper and then sell it to the ultimate provider of funds. These firms are commercial banks, finance companies, and savings institutions. As shown in Figure 6-4, the market shares of the $26 billion manufactured home loan market are pretty evenly aportioned among these three classes of lenders.

---

3 Manufactured home, rather than mobile home, has become the preferred terminology recently.

In addition to these lenders, some firms operate as mortgage bankers, buying the loans from manufactured home dealers or from banks and finance companies and then selling them in the secondary market. The primary purchaser of FHA/VA mobile home loans is Ginnie Mae.

Since 1973, Ginnie Mae has pooled and packaged FHA/VA mobile home loans for resale as securities. (GNMA uses the term "mobile home" rather than "manufactured home.") GNMA mobile home securities are similar to GNMA mortgage pass-throughs. The timely payment of principal and interest on mobile-home securities is guaranteed by the full faith and credit of the United States through Ginnie Mae. As of June 1988, about $3 billion of GNMA pass-throughs collateralized by mobile home loans were outstanding, representing only one percent of all GNMA pass-throughs.[4]

About half, $1.5 billion, of the GNMA mobile home pass-throughs outstanding are "in default."[5] "In default," according to Ginnie Mae, means that the originator/servicer could not pass-through monthly principal and interest. Therefore, some loans "in default" are delinquent, not defaulted. One reason for the high default/delinquency rate is that FHA loans outnumber VA loans about two to one and FHA loans carry a noncomprehensive guarantee. Many FHA lenders have used up their 10-percent pool insurance limit.

In the private sector, Green Tree Acceptance Corporation is the only issuer of publicly offered securities backed by manufactured housing loans. Green Tree, a Minnesota-based corporation, purchases, pools, sells, and services loans for manufactured housing as well as loans for recreational vehicles. Green Tree is the largest servicer of conventional manufactured housing loans, and as of June 1988, the company had securitized over $400 million in manufactured housing loans. In September 1987 Green Tree sold its first public issue

---

4 Government National Mortgage Association.
5 Government National Mortgage Association.

of pass-through securities backed by manufactured housing loans, and as of June 1988, the company had securitized over $400 million in manufactured housing loans.

Figure 6-4   Market Share of Mobile Home Loans Outstanding (Year End 1987)

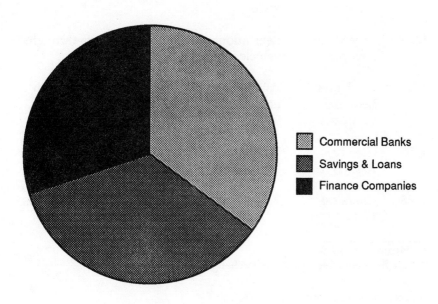

Source: Board of Governors of the Federal Reserve System.

Other Installment Loans

In addition to auto loans, credit card receivables, and loans for manufactured homes, other consumer installment loans have been securitized. As shown in Table 6-2, unsecured consumer loans, loans to finance the purchase of recreational vehicles and pleasure boats, policyholder loans, and time-sharing loans have been securitized.

**Table 6-2   The Securitization of Other Consumer Loans
(Selected Issues)**

	Issuer	Type of Asset	$Millions	Type of Security
11/87	Household Bank FSB	Secured and unsecured consumer loans	$432.0	Pay-through note
12/87	Green Tree Acceptance*	Recreational vehicle loans	25.0	Pass-throughs
2/88	Prudential Insurance Company	Policy-holder loans	440.0	Pay-through note
4/88	Glen Ivy Resorts*	Time-sharing loans	29.0	Pass-throughs
6/88	Chemical Bank**	Boat loans	200.0	Pass-throughs

---

* Private placement.
** Date filed with Securities and Exchange Commission.

Source: *Asset Sales Report*, various issues.

The pass-through structure has been used to securitize loans for recreational vehicles (RVs) and pleasure craft as well as time-sharing loans. RV loans and boat loans are similar to auto loans and have been securitized in a similar manner. About $400 million in pass-through certificates backed by RV loans have been privately placed by Green Tree Acceptance Corporation, and in June 1988, Chemical Bank filed with the Securities and Exchange Commission to issue $200 million in securities backed by "marine retail installment sales contracts on new and used boats."

Time-sharing loans finance the purchase of an interest in a property. The interest entitles the owner to a limited stay (e.g., one week per year) in the property. While not the first issue to be privately placed, a $29-million issue of time-sharing pass-through certificates was sold for a California-based resort developer in April 1988. The average loan in the pool was for $7,000 and matured in eight years.

Utilizing the pay-through structure, unsecured consumer loans and policyholder loans have also been securitized.

In November 1987, Household Bank FSB, headquartered in California and a wholly-owned subsidiary of Household International, issued two classes of pay-through notes collateralized by a consumer loan pass-through certificate for $432 million. The first class matured in one year; the second, in three. The consumer loans that backed the certificate, were fixed-rate, level-pay, closed-end consumer loans that were either unsecured or secured by personal property. Household provided a limited 15-percent guarantee.

Pay-through notes backed by life insurance policyholder loans were issued by Prudential Insurance Company in February 1988. The $440 million private placement, dubbed "death-backed bonds," was collateralized by $609 million in policyholder loans. Such loans are made by insurance companies to their policyholders and collateralized by their insurance policies. Because the interest rate on these loans is generally very low, policyholders have little incentive to repay the loans. Therefore, a borrower makes only interest payments and upon his death, the unpaid balance is taken from his death benefits.

Government-Related Loans

The U.S. government has played a very large role in the development of asset securitization. As discussed in Chapter 3, the federal government guarantees some mortgage loans and mortgage securities. The federal government also guarantees a portion of some small business loans and securities backed by the guaranteed portion of these loans. Through such guarantee programs, the U.S. government has greatly encouraged the growth of the secondary markets for residential mortgage loans and small business loans. Recently, the government has laid the foundation to do the same for agricultural mortgage loans. In addition, since 1986 the U.S. government has been securitizing some of the loans originated by its departments and agencies. This section discusses the securitization of small business loans and farm mortgages guaranteed by the United States as well as the securitization of nonguaranteed government loans.

Small Business Loans

Small Business Administration (SBA) loans have been securitized since 1985. SBA loans, available to small businesses, are guaranteed by the SBA, an agency of the U.S. government. The SBA defines small business generally as a manufacturer or wholesaler that employs fewer than 1,500 people or a service firm or retailer that has gross revenues below $14.5 million. The SBA guarantees up to 90 percent of the loan amount for loans under $155,000 and up to 85 percent for loans in excess of $155,000, but the guarantee cannot exceed $500,000.

SBA loans are originated either directly by the SBA or indirectly by private lenders. Direct loans cannot exceed $150,000 and are available only to borrowers who are unable to obtain an SBA-guaranteed loan through a private lender. Funds for direct loans are limited and sometimes available only to certain types of borrowers.

Direct SBA loans are originated by private lenders, such as commercial banks. A private lender initially reviews the loan application of a small business and, upon approval, submits it to the SBA. If approved by the SBA, the private lender closes the loan and disburses the funds.

Over the last eight years, about $1.5 billion of SBA loans were originated annually.[6] The average size of an SBA loan is about $100,000. Loans for working capital have maturities of between five and seven years, while loans for fixed assets or major renovations have longer maturities. The maximum maturity of an SBA loan is 25 years. The interest rate on SBA loans is no more than 275 basis points over New York prime for loans that mature in seven years or more and no more than 225 basis points over New York prime for loans that mature in less than seven years. SBA loans are usually collateralized. The collateral is assets of the small business and, if these assets are insufficient, liens on the personal property of the small business' owner may be required.

In July 1984, the Small Business Secondary Market Improvements Act authorized the SBA to establish a program for securitizing SBA loans similar to that of GNMA (see Table 6-3). In August 1985 the SBA issued guidelines for SBA pools. These guidelines standardized SBA lending and, therefore, made pooling easier. According to the guidelines, the assets in the pools must be the guaranteed portion of loans guaranteed under the Small Business Act (i.e., SBA loans), and no loan in a pool could be more than 29 days past due. In addition, each pool had to consist of at least four loans, and no loan could account for more than 25 percent of the face value of a pool. The minimum pool amount is $1 million. The minimum certificate size is $25,000, and all certificates must be in multiples of $5,000 except for one-certificate pools. The "pool rate" (pass-through rate) must be equal to the lowest rate net of fees on an individual loan in the pool, and the interest rates on loan in a pool must be within two percent of each other. The shortest maturity of a loan in a pool must be 70 percent or more of the loan with the longest remaining maturity. Pools should consist of all fixed-rate loans or all floating-rate loans. If the rates are floating, they must float on the same basis.

---

6 Small Business Administration.

Table 6-3   Small Business Administration Pooling Guidelines

Assets in Pool:
- Guaranteed portion of SBA loans
- No loan more than 29 days past due

Pool Characteristics:
- At least four loans to a pool
- No loan can account for more than 25% of pool amount
- Minimum pool size is $ 1 million
- Loans must have interest rates within 2% of each other
- The shortest maturity of a loan in a pool must be no less than 70% of the longest maturity
- Floating rate loans must float on same basis

Securities
- Minimum denomination of $25,000
- Denominations in multiples of $5,000
- Pool interest rate must equal the lowest rate on a loan in the pool

Source: Small Business Administration

Securities backed by SBA loans are similar to GNMA pass-throughs. Like Ginnie Mae, the SBA is not the issuer of the securities; the pool assemblers are. Pool assemblers must be regulated financial entities such as commercial banks, S&Ls, insurance companies, and broker/dealers. Most pool assemblers are broker/dealers. Also, like Ginnie Mae, the SBA guarantees the timely payment of principal and interest on the loan-backed securities.

The first SBA asset-backed securities were sold in August 1985, and in February 1986, First National Bank of Wisconsin became the first bank to package SBA loans and sell them as securities. As of April 1988, over 500 pools, representing about

$1.5 billion of SBA loan-backed securities had been sold to investors.[7]

Farmer Mac

The 1987 Agricultural Credit Act provided for the creation of the Federal Agriculture Mortgage Corporation. The corporation, dubbed Farmer Mac, is expected to be operational by mid-1989.

It will operate much like Ginnie Mae and the SBA's secondary market program. Farmer Mac will standardize the underwriting, appraisal, and repayment of loans that are eligible for the secondary market program; establish eligibility requirements for and certify individual financial institutions as pool assemblers of agricultural mortages; and guarantee timely payment of principal and interest on qualified pools of agricultural mortgages sold in the secondary market.

In addition to Farmer Mac's guarantee, which is supported by a $1.5 billion line of credit from the U.S. Treasury, credit enhancement will be provided by 10-percent overcollateralization provided by the pool assemblers. Cash flows from the excess collateral is used to establish a reserve fund, and the balances in the reserve fund will be used to pay any losses prior to using the Treasury line of credit.

Nonguaranteed Government Loans

So far the discussion of securitization has concerned loans originated in the private sector, but the public sector, i.e., the goverment, holds a substantial amount of loans. The U.S. government has a loan portfolio in excess of $200 billion.[8] The recipients of most of these loans are small businesses, students,

---

7 Small Business Administration.

8 Board of Governors of the Federal Reserve System, *Flow of Funds Accounts Financial Assets and Liabilites Year-End, 1964-87.*

farmers, and other borrowers who could not obtain credit elsewhere.

In 1986, the Reagan administration issued guidelines to be followed by federal departments and agencies in raising over $5 billion by selling loans without recourse and without a guarantee during fiscal 1987. The government expected to receive, on average, 50 cents for every dollar of loans sold.

During fiscal year 1987 and most of fiscal year 1988, the U.S. Departments of Agriculture, Education, Health and Urban Development as well as the SBA and the Veterans Administration raised nearly $5 billion from the sale of $7.3 billion in assets. Most of the loans sold were for housing projects and for public works projects, and many were sold as asset-backed securities. For example, one issue of government loan-backed bonds was a $1.8 billion issue backed by tax-exempt water and sewer project loans. Another issue was a $127-million issue of bonds backed by Department of Education loans to small universities and colleges for the construction of housing and buildings.

Commercial Loans

Commercial loans certainly have not been securitized as frequently as consumer loans. Commercial loans other than SBA loans, however, have been securitized. Trade receivables, loans for employee stock ownership plans, premium loans, leveraged buyout loans, and nonguaranteed small business loans have been pooled and repackaged as securities (Table 6-4). The securitization of these assets has predominantly been in the form of asset-backed bonds, although the pay-through and pass-through structures have also been used. In addition, facilities have been established that, in effect, securitized the commercial loans of banks.

Trade Receivables

Trade receivables have been securitized as asset-backed commercial paper, asset-backed preferred stock, and asset-backed notes, along the same lines as asset-backed bonds. The receivables were sold to special-purpose corporations, which fund the purchase of the receivables by issuing securities. AMAX, a metals and mining company, first securitized trade receivables in 1982 by issuing asset-backed commercial paper that was enhanced with an insurance bond. Associated Grocers, a Seattle-based distributor of wholesale grocery items, also issued asset-backed securities backed by trade-related receivables. In February 1988, the firm issued floating-rate certificates backed by the accounts receivable of retailers who bought groceries and supermarket equipment from Associated.

In 1987, Mattel (a toy manufacturer) and Union Carbide (a chemical company) issued asset-backed preferred stock via special purpose corporations. The cash flows from the receivables were used to make dividend payments and to redeem shares. These firms issued asset-backed preferred stock rather than asset-backed bonds because their effective tax rates were not high enough to take full advantage of the interest deductions from debt financing.

**Table 6-4 The Securitization of Commercial Loans
(Selected Issues)**

	Issuer	Type of Asset	$Millions	Type of Security
9/87	Mattel, Inc.	Trade receivables	$62.5	Preferred stock
9/87	Union Carbide	Trade receivables	249.0	Preferred stock
10/87	Cannanwill, Inc.*	Premium loans	160.0	Euronotes
12/87	Allied Signal*	ESOP loans	6.0	Notes
2/88	Citicorp*	Loans to McDonald's franchisees	29.0	Pass-throughs

*Private placement

Source: *Asset Sales Report*, various issues.

Other Commercial-Type Loans

In addition to trade receivables, premium loans and loans for employee stock ownership plans (ESOPs) have been securitized as asset-backed bonds. In October 1987, $160 million in Euronotes backed by premium loans were sold for a subsidiary of an insurance holding company. Premium loans are made to companies for them to pay their property/casualty insurance premiums. Less than ten firms are major originators of this type of loan and most are captive finance subsidiaries of insurance companies.

ESOPs are contributory benefit programs that companies set up for their employees. Usually, when a firm establishes an ESOP, it buys all the stock for the plan at one time. The stock is then allocated to employees over several years. Commercial banks have routinely sold participations in ESOP loans, but lately they have been pooling them and selling credit-enhanced securities backed by the ESOP loans. ESOP-backed notes have been issued privately as floating-rate notes with maturities of about seven years. As of September 1988, nearly $1 billion of ESOP loans had been securitized.

While trade receivables, premium loans, and ESOP loans have been sold essentially as asset-backed bonds, leveraged buyout (LBO) loans have been sold as pay-through notes, and participations have been sold in LBO portfolios. LBO loans, which are often sold as participations, were first securitized in October 1988. At that time, Manufacturers Hanover Trust Company sold participations in a fund consisting of new LBO credits, which it had set up several months earlier. In November, Continental Illinois Bank and Trust Company issued two classes of pay-through notes backed by seasoned LBO loans.

One very particular type of small business loan has also been sold as pay-through notes and pass-through certificates. In February 1988, $29 million of loans to McDonald's restaurant franchisees were securitized as pass-through certificates. The loans were fixed-rate loans with five to seven year maturities. The pass-throughs were credit-enhanced by a spread account.[9] Later, in April 1988, similar loans were securitized as pay-through notes.

While specific types of commercial loans have been securitized, the securitization of loans for working capital and fixed assets has only very recently been accomplished by two firms.

Diversified Financial Corporation (formerly Dimensional Financial Corporation) had tried without success to sell participations in a diversified pool of commercial loans until 1988 when it created Diversified Corporate Loans Inc., which will serve as an exchange and auction for conforming commercial loans. Sellers can sell loans into a pool of commercial loans and buyers can buy participations in the pool at the day's prevailing spread. The loan originators continue to service the loans and remit the loan payments to DCL's depository. The company is expected to be operational by year-end 1988.

In mid-1988, Pilgrim Group Inc., a Los Angeles based mutual fund company, securitized commercial loans when it began to sell shares in a fund that invests in collateralize bank loans made by money center and large regional banks to domestic companies. The shares are sold to retail customers, and as of November 1988, the fund had about $115 million in assets.

Some Conclusions

In chapter 1, the following question was asked: Can everything be securitized? The answer was, "Probably not." Nevertheless, since 1985, when automobile loans were first pooled, repackaged and sold as securities, many other types of assets have been securitized (see Table 6-5). As of June 1988, over 10 types of assets had been securitized as public offerings, and additional types of assets had been securitized and privately

---

9 See Chapter 2 for a discussion of spread accounts.

placed. While everything probably cannot be securitized, many types of assets can. The growth and development of asset securitization since 1985 indicates that the limits of securitization are by no means narrowly drawn.

Table 6-5 The Development of the Market
for Nonmortgage-Related Asset-Backed Securities

	No. of Issues	No. of Issuers	No. of New Issuers	Types of Assets
1985	7	6	6	2
1986	16	9	6	2
1987	37	22	18	9
1988 (June)	22	19	8	7

Source: *Asset Sales Report*, various issues.

PART III

▶ The Environment for ◀ Asset-Backed Securities

CHAPTER 7

Accounting for Securitization:
▶ GAAP versus RAP ◀

AS DISCUSSED IN CHAPTER 1, asset-backed securities usually take one of two legal forms. They represent either beneficial interests in a pool of assets—pass-through certificates—or debt obligations collateralized by a pool of assets—pay-through notes or asset-backed bonds. The legal form of an asset-backed security is a key determinant of its accounting treatment, but the accounting treatment also plays a crucial role in determining whether a pool of assets is securitized as debt or as ownership interest.

Two sets of principles govern the accounting of securitization—generally accepted accounting principles (GAAP) used in published financial statements and regulatory accounting principles (RAP) used in Call Reports and other regulatory financial reports used by supervisory agencies. The Securities and Exchange Commission has the legal authority to set accounting conventions used in financial statements of publicly held corporations; the SEC has delegated this authority to the standards setting organizations recognized by the accounting profession. Currently, it is delegated to the Financial Accounting Standards Board (FASB).

RAP is set by the regulatory agencies of depository institutions and governs the accounting practices of commercial banks and savings institutions. For federally-insured commercial banks, RAP is set by the Federal Reserve Board, the Federal Deposit Insurance Corporation, and the Office of the Comptroller of the Currency through the Federal Financial Institutions Examination Council.[1] Savings institutions follow GAAP with respect to securitized asset transactions. Although the regulatory agencies try to keep RAP consistent with GAAP whenever possible, their supervisory responsibilities sometimes dictate limited departures from GAAP. For federally-insured commercial banks, RAP and GAAP are essentially the same in the vast majority of cases. However, GAAP and RAP differ in some respects, including their treatment of securitization. Thus, the same transaction may have to be accounted for differently under RAP and GAAP.

Although they differ, both GAAP and RAP have one main question at the heart of their treatment of asset securitization: Does the transaction constitute a sale or a borrowing (pledge of assets as collateral)? After explaining why accounting treatment is important to the structure of asset-backed securities, this chapter examines the rules for determining whether a transaction gives rise to a sale of assets or a borrowing under GAAP and RAP and discusses their implications for financial statements and for regulation. This chapter also discusses the rules for consolidating separate issuing entities. A comparison of GAAP and RAP is also provided.

---

1 The Federal Reserve Board permits bank holding companies to use GAAP in financial reports filed with the Board under Regulation Y.

Why Accounting Treatment Matters

The accounting treatment of asset securitization will matter to an issuer (seller) if the issuer is concerned with its own financial leverage and profitability. If the securitization of assets qualifies for sale treatment, the issuer will probably be able to reduce its leverage and increase its return on assets and return on equity. Furthermore, if the issuer is a depository institution (an S&L or a commercial bank), sale treatment under RAP will allow the issuer to reduce its regulatory taxes, i.e., foregone interest income on required reserves held at the Federal Reserve, deposit insurance premiums, and capital requirements in excess of capital that would be held in the absence of regulation.[2]

Table 7-1 shows how securitization can increase a firm's profitability and how accounting treatment that recognizes a sale of assets is preferable to treatment that recognizes a transaction as a collateralized borrowing. In the hypothetical example in Table 7-1, a transaction that qualifies as a sale would increase the seller's reported return on assets by 35 basis points and its return on equity by at least 333 basis points over a comparable transaction reported as a borrowing. If the seller were a depository institution, the sale of assets would also save roughly 52 basis points in regulatory taxes.[3]

---

2 Because returns to equity holders are taxable, and returns to debtholders are treated as an expense and therefore tax-deductible, equity is a more expensive funding source than debt, and requiring banks to hold more capital than would be demanded of an unregulated financial institution drives up the cost of funding.

3 Herbert Baer and Christine Pavel, "Does regulation drive innovation?" *Economic Perspectives*, Federal Reserve Bank of Chicago (March/April 1988.)

Table 7-1 Implications of Accounting Treatment

	Pre-Sale	Maintain Leverage After Sale	Maintain Leverage After Borrowing	Purchase/Originate New Loans After Sale	Purchase/Originate New Loans After Borrowing
Assets					
Auto loans (12%)	100	--	100	100	200
Other loans (12%)	900	900	900	900	900
	1000	900	1000	1000	1100
Liabilities					
Deposits (6%)	940	846	940	940	1040
Equity	60	54	60	60	60
	1000	900	1000	1000	1100
Income					
Interest	102	90	102	102	114
Servicing (8%)	--	8	--	8	--
	102	98	102	110	114
Expenses					
Interest (6%)	56.4	50.8	56.4	56.4	62.4
Servicing (3%)	30.0	30.0	30.0	33.0	33.0
	86.4	80.8	86.4	89.4	95.4
Net Income	15.6	17.2	15.6	20.6	18.6
ROA	1.56%	1.91%	1.56%	2.06%	1.69%
ROE	26.00%	31.85%	26.00%	34.33%	31.00%

Sales Versus Borrowings

As illustrated in the example above, a sale of assets is usually preferable to additional borrowings.[4] But what factors determine whether a transaction qualifies as a sale?

A transaction constitutes a sale if assets are sold to a third-party without recourse and without retention of any residual interest in the assets. The assets are then eliminated from the seller's balance sheet, and any resulting gains or losses are recorded at that time. This is true under both GAAP and RAP. If, however, assets are sold to a third-party with recourse, the accounting treatment under GAAP and RAP differs.

Under GAAP, these transactions would be accounted for in accordance with FASB Statement 77 or FASB Technical Bulletin 85-2. Some securitized asset transactions, however, may not be covered directly under these pronouncements and, therefore, must be accounted for using the guidance contained in them by analogy.

Asset Sales with Recourse Under GAAP

Statement of Financial Accounting Standards No. 77 (FAS77) establishes the accounting standards for transfers of assets with recourse that "purport to be sales of receivables." "Recourse" is defined in FAS77 as the right of a purchaser of receivables to receive payment from the seller of those receivables for "failure of the debtors to pay when due, the effects of prepayments, or adjustments resulting from defects in the eligibility of the transferred receivables."[5] If, however, the seller guarantees the buyer against loss from both prepayments and late payments

---

4 If it is important to the issuer to retain the tax benefits of the assets, then a collateralized borrowing may be preferable to a sale.

5 Financial Accounting Standards Board, *Statement of Financial Accounting Standards No. 77, Reporting by Transferors for Transfers of Receivables with Recourse,* December 1983.

as well as defaults, the transaction, in effect, would be "a borrowing with fixed repayment terms that should not be accounted for as a sale."[6]

According to FAS77, a transfer of assets with recourse is recognized as a sale if all of the following criteria are met:

- The transferor surrenders control of the future economic benefits embodied in the receivables. If the transferor has an option to repurchase the receivables at a later date, a sale cannot be recorded. However, a right of first refusal based on a bona fide offer by an unrelated third party ordinarily is not considered a repurchase option.

- The transferor's obligation under the recourse provisions can be reasonably estimated. A transfer of receivables cannot be recognized as a sale if the costs of the recourse provisions are not subject to reasonable estimation.

- The transferee cannot require the transferor to repurchase the receivables except pursuant to the recourse provisions. However, "clean-up calls," or options to repurchase the receivables when the remaining uncollected balance is very small in order to keep the costs of servicing the receivables to reasonable levels, are allowed.

If any of the above conditions is not met, the transaction should be reported as a borrowing and the proceeds from the transfer of assets should be reported as a liability.

If the conditions for sale treatment under FAS77 are met, the assets sold are eliminated from the issuer's (seller's) balance sheet. At the date of sale, the seller must record all probable adjustments arising from the recourse provisions. Probable adjustments include adjustments for probable credit losses arising

---

6 Raymond E. Perry and Peter J. Krolak, "Securitized Asset Structures," Touche Ross, 1987.

from the recourse provisions, effects of prepayments, and defects in the eligibility of transferred receivables.

If the seller retains the servicing and will not be paid a separate servicing fee in future periods, part of the original proceeds from the sale represents a fee for servicing and should be deferred at the date of sale. Consequently, the sales price should be adjusted to provide for a normal servicing fee in each subsequent servicing period. If, however, the transaction provides the seller with servicing fees that exceed the normal rate, the present value of excess future servicing fees should be recorded as an "other asset" and additional sales proceeds at the time of sale.

For transfers of receivables with recourse that are reported as sales, the sellers' financial statements must disclose the proceeds to the seller for each income statement period and the balance of the transferred receivables that remain uncollected at the date of each balance sheet, if the information is available. In addition, even if losses from a recourse provision have not been incurred, the guarantor (seller) should disclose the recourse provision in its financial statements. The disclosure should "include the nature and amount of the guarantee, [and] if estimable, the value of any recovery that could be expected."[7] If loss from a recourse provision occurs, the loss from the provision should be charged against the recourse liability that was recorded at the date of sale.

Collateralized Borrowings Under GAAP

If the legal form of asset-backed securities is debt and the assets collateralizing the securities are mortgage loans or participations in pools of mortgage loans, then FASB Technical Bulletin No. 85-2 (TB85-2) dictates whether the issuance of such

---

7 Financial Accounting Standards Board, *Statement of Financial Accounting Standards No. 5, Accounting for Contingencies,* March 1975.

securities will be treated as a sale of the assets that collateralize the securities or as a borrowing.[8] Although TB85-2 specifically addresses the accounting for bonds secured by mortgage loans or mortgage-backed securities, its conditions could also be applied to structures involving debt collateralized by other assets, although there is not agreement on this point.[9]

While FAS77, in some instances, allows for sale treatment even if assets are sold with recourse, TB85-2 generally prohibits sale treatment if the transaction even hints of recourse. According to TB85-2, sale treatment is warranted if all the following conditions are met:

- Neither the issuer nor its affiliates have the right or obligation to substitute collateral or obtain it by calling the obligation. (Clean-up calls, however, are permitted.)

- The expected residual interest in the collateral, computed by using the present value of all amounts expected to revert to the issuer or its affiliates, including reinvestment earnings, is nominal (insignificant). Excess servicing fees sould be considered to be part of the expected residual interest.

- The investor can look only to the issuer's assets or third parties (such as insurers or guarantors) for repayment of both principal and interest on the obligation, and neither the sponsor of the issuer nor its other affiliates are secondarily liable.

- Neither the issuer nor its affiliates can be required to redeem the obligation prior to its stated maturity other than through the normal pay-through of collections from the collateral.

---

8 Financial Accounting Standards Board, *Technical Bulletin No. 85-2, Accounting for Collateralized Mortgage Obligations (CMOs)*, March 18, 1985.
9 Touche Ross.

If the conditions for sale treatment under TB85-2 are met, the assets used as collateral are eliminated from the issuer's balance sheet, and any expected residual interest in the collateral is not recognized as an asset but rather recorded as it accrues to the benefit of the issuer. If servicing is retained by an affiliate of the issuer for a fee that is less than normal, the bond proceeds should be adjusted to reflect a normal servicing fee in subsequent periods. All transaction costs associated with the offering should be charged to expenses when the associated collateral is eliminated from the financial statements.

Bank Regulatory Accounting Principles

While the criteria for GAAP are based on the transfer of benefits, the criteria for sale treatment under bank regulatory accounting principles are based on the transfer of risk. Although a key factor under FAS77 is the ability to estimate the risk retained, "the existence of risk" is what is important for supervisory and regulatory purposes.

As mentioned above, if assets are sold without recourse, they are eliminated from the seller's balance sheet under both GAAP and RAP. If a bank sells assets with recourse, under GAAP it can eliminate those assets from its balance sheet as long as it can reasonably estimate the costs of the recourse provision; however, under RAP the bank must retain the assets on its books and it must treat the transaction as a borrowing. Therefore, it must hold the required proportion of capital against the assets and it may have to maintain reserves at the Fed against the proceeds from the "sale."

Thus, securitization of assets raises two questions under RAP. First, if a bank sells securitized assets with recourse, does it have to keep the assets on its books and hold capital against them, and if so, how much? Second, are the proceeds from the sale of securitized assets with an obligation to repurchase some or all of the assets considered deposits, and does a bank have to hold reserves against the proceeds?

Capital Requirements

For commercial banks, the Federal Reserve Board, the Federal Deposit Insurance Corporation, and the Office of the Comptroller of the Currency set policy with regard to the first question—capital requirements on assets sold with recourse. For bank holding companies, the Federal Reserve Board sets capital policy.

The question of capital requirements arises because securitization that involves the sale of assets reduces the assets of a bank, but leaves the riskiness of a bank unchanged if the bank agrees to buy back all or a portion of the portfolio of underlying loans in the event of default, or if the bank guarantees the payment of principal and interest on securities. If the bank guarantees the securities, it still assumes the risk of the underlying loans. Therefore, should a bank have to hold capital against the sale of securitized assets if the securities are somehow guaranteed by the bank, and if so, how much?

According to the Federal Reserve Board's Instructions for Preparation of Consolidated Financial Statements of Bank Holding Companies, the sale of assets should be reported "in accordance with generally accepted accounting principles." Bank holding companies, however, must disclose the "net impact on total assets, retained earnings, and net income of assets that were 'sold' (but that are still outstanding) with any retention of risk."

Commercial banks, however, generally must hold capital against assets sold with recourse. According to instructions for filing the Reports of Condition and Income, "a transfer of loans, securities, receivables, or other assets is to be reported as a sale of the transferred assets" by the selling institution and a purchase by the purchasing institution *"only* if the selling institution retains no risk of loss from the sale of assets and has no obligation to any party to pay principal or interest on the assets sold." Thus, "if risk of loss or obligation for payment of principal or interest is retained by, or may fall back upon, the seller, the transaction *must* be reported by the seller as a borrowing from the purchaser and by the purchaser as a loan to the seller." The selling institution must keep the assets on its books and include them in its calculation of capital requirements.

The Call Report instructions list the following five specific cases where risk would be retained by the selling institution and, therefore, the transaction would be reported as a borrowing:

- The sale of an asset with a realistic bona fide put option allowing the purchaser, at its option, to return the asset to the seller.

- The sale or an asset guaranteed by a standby letter of credit issued by the seller.

- The sale of an asset guaranteed by a standby letter of credit issued by any other party in which risk, either directly or indirectly, rests with the seller.

- The sale of an asset guaranteed by an insurance contract in which the seller, either directly or indirectly, indemnifies or otherwise protects the issuer in any manner against loss.

- The sale of a short-term loan under a long-term commitment (a so-called "strip participation").

Provisions that allow for the return of assets because of fraud or incomplete documentation do not qualify as recourse provisions. Also, the retention of an interest in a spread account does not in and of itself constitute recourse.[10]

Another exception involves provisions that guarantee a specific percentage of losses. If the selling institution promises to compensate purchasers for losses up to a certain percentage of the value of the assets sold or a specific dollar amount, the entire amount of the assets must be reported and carried on the

---

10 Federal Financial Institutions Examination Council, Press Release, November 21, 1986.

seller's books, and the proceeds from the transaction must be reported as a borrowing; however, if the selling institution guarantees a percentage of the losses, rather than a percentage of the value of the assets, the seller is required to hold a reduced amount of capital if no other provisions exist that result in the retention of risk by the seller, either directly or indirectly. In that case, the seller would only have to report that percentage of losses times the sales proceeds received from the assets sold on its balance sheet. Thus, for example, if a bank sold $1 million of auto loans and promised to compensate purchasers for losses up to 10 percent of the portfolio, the bank would have to continue to report the entire $1 million as assets on its balance sheet and continue to hold roughly $55,000 of capital against these loans.[11] But if the bank guaranteed 10 percent of the default losses incurred on the portfolio, the bank would remove $900,000 of assets from its balance sheet, report $100,000 as a borrowing, and hold $5,500 of capital against these loans (assuming, in this example, that sales proceeds equals the carrying amount of the assets).

The regulatory accounting principles discussed above do not apply to the sale of pass-through pools of residential mortgages. If a financial institution sells mortgages under a GNMA, FNMA, or FHLMC program, the transaction is treated as a sale of assets (which are removed from the balance sheet), but the reporting of privately-issued mortgage-backed securities depends on the retention of risk. "Only when the issuing bank does not retain any significant risk of loss, either directly or indirectly, is the transaction to be reported as a sale of the underlying mortgages by the issuing bank." Significant risk is not defined, and each of the three bank regulatory agencies has a different view on what consititutes "significant."

If a transaction qualifies for sale treatment under RAP, the seller eliminates the assets from its balance sheet and recognizes any gains or losses. If the transaction involves passing through to the purchaser an interest rate that is lower than that

---

11 This assumes a required capital-to-asset ratio of 5.5 percent.

stated on the asset sold, after adjusting for a normal servicing fee, the gain on the sale resulting from the differential is reported as it is realized over the life of the asset sold. This treatment is in contrast to that under FAS77, where the present value of "excess servicing" is recognized as an immediate gain. Under RAP, however, if the pass-through rate is greater than the stated rate on the asset sold, the seller must recognize the loss immediately.

Reserve Requirements

The treatment of asset sales for purposes of reserve requirements is not entirely consistent with their treatment for capital requirements. Consequently, a transaction may give rise to a borrowing for purposes of the Call Report, but the proceeds from that borrowing may not be reservable.

The question of reservability was formally addressed in 1983 by the Federal Reserve Board's Legal Division in response to banks' sales of industrial revenue bonds (IRBs). Because of poor earnings, banks were not able to profit from tax-exempt income. Consequently, they were selling IRBs with an unconditional obligation to repurchase the bonds in the event of default. The Board's legal staff said:

> For purposes of Regulation D, the sale of the loans subject to an unconditional agreement to repurchase is properly regarded as a borrowing by the bank . . . [We] continue to be of the view that the bank's obligation to repurchase gives rise to the creation of a deposit.[12]

There have been exceptions to this rule. First, Regulation D states that a deposit does not include "an obligation arising from the retention by a depository institution of no more than a

---

12 Gilbert T. Schwartz, letter to Reserve Bank General Counsels. March 7, 1983.

10 percent interest in a pool of conventional one-to-four-family mortgages that are sold to third parties." Thus, if a bank issues mortgage pass-through securities and promises to compensate purchasers for losses up to 10 percent of the market value of the underlying pool of mortgage loans at the time of sale, the proceeds from the sale of the pass-throughs are not considered deposits. Therefore, they are not reservable. This 10-percent rule, however, applies only to mortgage pass-through securities and does not extend to securities backed by a pledge of mortgages or other types of assets, nor to other asset sales. The Fed allows the proceeds from pass-throughs to be exempt from reserve requirements in order to encourage the growth of the secondary mortgage market.[13]

A second exception was made by Board staff for asset sales with recourse in 1980. A bank proposed to sell IRBs with a guarantee provided by an independent insurance company. The bank paid a premium for the guarantee, but the bank also agreed to indemnify the insurer for any losses incurred as a result of the bonds. The purchasers of the bonds knew only that the insurance company guaranteed the bonds; they were not aware of the agreement for reimbursement between the bank and the insurer. The Board's legal staff reasoned that "the insurance broke the nexus between the sale of the assets by the bank and the purchase of the assets by the third party. Thus, the bank's obligation was not regarded as issued in connection with the raising of funds."[14] Therefore, the proceeds from the sale of the IRBs were not considered deposits and were not reservable in the 1980 case.

As asset sales and securitization of nonmortgage assets became more common, the Federal Reserve Board received numerous requests for interpretations of Regulation D, especially with regard to the reservability of asset sales with recourse by depository institutions. Consequently, in May

---

13 Federal Financial Institutions Examination Council, memo, October 28, 1987.

14 Letter from Gilbert T. Schwartz of March 7, 1983.

1986, the Board issued for comment a proposal to clarify Regulation D by amending the definition of "deposit." This proposed amendment would define "deposit" to include "sales of assets where the depository institution issues or undertakes a liability supporting the assets sold or retains a reversionary interest in these assets, regardless of whether the liability or interest is conditional, unconditional or contingent or whether the liability covers all or a portion of the assets sold."[15] The proposal would preserve the Board's earlier exception to the definition of "deposit" for sales with recourse of one-to-four-family mortgage pools where the seller retains no more than a 10-percent interest in the pool.

While the Board's proposal would not extend this exception to other types of assets, it does provide for a few exceptions to the definition of "deposit" for other types of assets sold with some kind of investor protection. First, if a depository institution sells an asset and agrees to be liable for 75 percent or less of the losses from that asset as they are realized, then, under the proposal, the proceeds from the asset sales would not be reservable. This treatment is not entirely consistent with the treatment of sharing in losses that is prescribed in the Call Report instructions; the Call Report instructions do not place a cap on the percentage of losses that the seller can share.

Second, the proposal would continue the former treatment of sales by a depository institution of assets that are guaranteed by a third party, and the "depository institution's only liability in the transaction is to reimburse a third-party guarantor of the assets sold." The proceeds from such a transaction would generally not be considered deposits under the Board's proposal. This treatment contrasts with that prescribed in the Call Report instructions, where "the sale of an asset guaranteed by an insurance contract in which the seller . . . indemnifies or otherwise protects the insurer in any manner against loss" qualifies as recourse and therefore is indicative of a borrowing.

---

15 Board of Governors of the Federal Reserve System, 12 CFR Par 204, May 1, 1986.

A transaction involving the "sale" of assets, therefore, can create a liability for purposes of the Call Report, but not necessarily a reservable liability.

Finally, the proposal would also exclude obligations of affiliates from the definition of deposits "if the proceeds from an affiliate's obligation are used to purchase assets from a depository institution without recourse"; the proposal would extend the definition of "affiliate" to include any organization that a depository institution effectively manages or controls. Currently Regulation D regards obligations of affiliates as deposits when the obligation would have been a deposit if it had been issued by the institution.

Regardless of whether or not an asset sold with recourse meets the above exceptions, the proceeds from the asset sale still might not be reservable under the current proposal if the maturity of the "liability" (that is, the recourse provision) is greater than 18 months. The Fed proposes to determine the maturity according to the remaining maturity of the assets sold unless the maturity is effectively shortened by the nature of the assets or the guarantee. The Fed is considering setting the maturity at the "earliest time" the guarantee could be exercised.

The key question with respect to the maturity would be "how soon does the seller have to come up with the money under the recourse provision?" If the answer is "immediately," then the borrowing would be considered a demand deposit reservable at 12 percent. If the answer is "seven days or more," then the borrowing would be considered a nonpersonal time deposit reservable at three percent. Even if the effective maturity was determined to be one day, the reserve requirements on an asset could be minimal if payments to the purchaser in the first 18 months primarily consist of interest payments, as reserves would apply only to the principal repaid in the first 18 months.

As of December 1988, the proposal to amend Regulation D had not become policy. However, because the portion of the proposal that defines deposit is merely a *clarification* of existing regulation, the Fed is defining deposits in accordance with the proposal. The portion of the proposal that redefines "affiliate" represents changes to existing regulation and, therefore, is not the current definition being used.

Consolidation

As discussed in Chapter 2, the seller of assets that are securitized often is not the issuer of the asset-backed securities. The issuer, for example, may be an issuing vehicle such as a grantor trust or a special-purpose corporation. Therefore, the question of consolidation arises. That is, if the securitization of assets cannot be treated as a sale by the issuer, does the issuing vehicle have to be consolidated with its parent?

The general rules for consolidation require consolidation of a majority-owned subsidiary unless control is likely to be temporary or if it does not rest with the majority owner.[16] If the issuance of asset-backed securities qualifies as a sale under FAS77 or under TB85-2, then the consolidation question does not arise because the issuer will have removed the assets from its balance sheet. If, however, the transaction does not qualify for sale treatment, then the issuer must be consolidated with the parent if a majority of it is owned by the parent. Majority ownership is usually determined by equity shares, but in multi-class structures, the residual interest is generally considered to be equity.

GAAP Versus RAP

Regulatory accounting principles are usually more restrictive than generally accepted accounting principles with respect to the securitization of assets as pass-through securities when the issuer (seller) guarantees the underlying assets or the securities (see Table 7-2). RAP and GAAP are almost equally restrictive

---

16 Financial Accounting Standard Board, *Statement of Financial Accounting Standard No. 94, Consolidation of All Majority-Owned Subsidiaries,* 1987.

with respect to the securitization of assets as pay-through bonds or asset-backed bonds.

Asset-backed securities that represent beneficial interests in a pool of assets, when the issuer guarantees all or a portion of the assets or securities, are usually afforded more favorable accounting treatment under GAAP than under RAP. According to RAP, unless the asset-backed securities are residential mortgage pass-throughs, especially federal agency pass-throughs, any retention of risk will require that at least some portion of the assets sold remain on the seller's balance sheet, and depending on the maturity of the asset-backed securities, the proceeds from the issuance of the asset-backed securities may be reservable. According to GAAP, however, if the retention of risk is estimable and the other criteria of FAS77 are met, then the issuer can report the transfer of assets as a sale and remove the assets from its balance sheet.

If the legal form of asset-backed securities is debt, then GAAP is only slightly less restrictive than RAP. The issuance of such securities would always be treated as a borrowing under RAP. Under GAAP there are certain conditions under which the issuance of collateralized debt could qualify for sale treatment. The conditions, however, are so restrictive that they are seldom met.

Table 7-2   Accounting for Securitization Under GAAP and RAP

	GAAP	*RAP*
Pass-Through Securities		
Sold without recourse	Sale of assets	Sale of assets
Nonmortgage securites with recourse		
• Recourse is estimable (e.g., auto securities)	Sale of assets	Borrowing
• Recourse is not estimable (e.g., commercial loans)	Borrowing	Borrowing
Mortgage securities with recourse		
• Federal agency securites	Sale of assets	Sale of assets
• Private securities	Sale of assets	depends on level of recourse
Pay-Through or Asset-Backed Securities		
Sustitution of collateral permitted and/or call option and/or early redemption permitted and/or residual interest more than "nominal"	Borrowing	Borrowing
No substitution of collateral and no call option and no early redemption permitted and residual interest "nominal"	Sale of assets	Borrowing

CHAPTER 8

▶ The Legal Environment ◀ for Asset-Backed Securities

SEVERAL FEDERAL STATUTES, state laws and Securities and Exchange Commission (SEC) rules affect the issuance of asset-backed securities. These laws and rules are primarily concerned with disclosure through registration and ongoing reporting requirements.

This chapter briefly discusses the Securities Act of 1933, Securities Exchange Act of 1934, Rule 415 under the Securities Act of 1933 and Exchange Commission's Rule 415, Investment Company Act of 1940, and blue sky (state-disclosure) laws. Emphasis is given to how these laws and rules affect asset-backed securities. A discussion of proposed legislation to encourage the development of the markets for certain non-mortgage-related asset-backed securities is provided at the end of the chapter.

Securities Act of 1933

The Securities Act of 1933 is primarily concerned with the initial public distribution of an issuer's securities rather than their subsequent trading. It is designed to provide investors with material information on publicly offered securities through registration and adequate disclosure. The 1933 Act is also concerned with prohibiting fraud in securities trading.

Under the Securities Act of 1933, securities offered publicly must be registered with the SEC unless they qualify for exemption. The term "securities" is defined to include bonds, debentures, evidences of indebtedness, and collateral-trust certificates as well as many other types of securities. What constitutes a public offering, or conversely a private placement, is prescribed in the SEC's Regulation D and in case law Regulation D, however provides a "safe harbor" for private placements.

Under Regulation D, an offering can qualify as a private placement in three ways. First, an offering of $500,000 or less qualifies as a private placement regardless of the number of purchasers. Second, an offering of less than $5 million sold to an unlimited number of sophisticated investors and no more than 35 other investors, where no general solicitation had taken place, also is considered a private placement. Third, any offering sold only to "accredited" investors and up to 35 sophisticated investors is considered a private placement. Accredited investors include, although not exclusively, banks, insurance companies, investment companies, and wealthy individuals.

The Securities Act of 1933 provides for other exemptions in addition to the one for privately placed securities. Such exemptions can be categorized as "class" exemptions and "transaction" exemptions. Class exemptions are concerned with certain types of securities, while transaction exemptions are concerned with certain types of transactions. The exemption of U.S. government securities and the securities of state and political subdivisions is an example of a class exemption. The exemption of securities that are privately placed is an example of a transaction exemption.

In 1975, the Congress amended the 1933 Act to encourage the development of the secondary mortgage market by providing a transaction exemption for mortgage-backed securities sold to sophisticated investors. This exemption applies to mortgage-backed securities that are originated by savings and loan associations or by banking institutions that are supervised and examined by federal or state authorities; it also applies to mortgages approved by the Secretary of Housing and Urban Development and sold to sophisticated investors rather than to the general investing public. No such exemption currently exists for non-mortgage-related asset-backed securities.

Securities or transactions that do not qualify for an exemption under the 1933 Act must be described by a registration statement filed with the Securities and Exchange Commission. The registration statement must include descriptions of the issuer's properties and business; descriptions of the securities being offered and their relationship to the issuer's other securities; the method by which the securities are to be distributed, along with information relating to the management of the issuer; and the issuer's financial statements, certified by an independent public accountant.

The Securities Exchange Act of 1934

The Securities Exchange Act of 1934 expands upon the disclosure requirements of the 1933 Act for securities of publicly held companies sold pursuant to an effective registration statement under the 1933 Act. Basically, the 1934 Act requires publicly held corporations to file annual, quarterly and other periodic reports with the Securities and Exchange Commission. The 1934 Act also empowers the Federal Reserve Board to prescribe the regulations for margin requirements, i.e., the amount of credit that may be initially extended and subsequently maintained on any security that is not exempt under the 1933 and 1934 Acts.

The Federal Reserve Board's Regulation T concerns margin requirements. According to Regulation T, a broker dealer may extend credit to a customer on the collateral of a corporate bond if the bond is either a registered security on a national securities exchange or an "OTC margin bond."

An OTC margin bond is defined as a bond that is not traded on a national securities exchange, but (1) it has a principal amount of $25 million or more outstanding at the time credit is extended; (2) it is registered under the Securities Act of 1933 and its issuer files periodic reports under the Securities Exchange Act of 1934 or is an insurance company according to the 1934 Act; and issuer, (3) the creditor, at the time of credit extension, has reasonable basis to believe that its issuer is not in default on the bond.

Similarly, a private mortgage pass-through security also qualifies as an OTC margin bond if the following conditions are met: (1) An aggregate principal amount of not less than $25 million was issued pursuant to a registration filed with the Securities and Exchange Commission under the Securities Act of 1933; (2) current reports to be filed with the SEC have been filed with the Commission; and (3) at the time of the credit extension, the creditor has reasonable basis to believe that mortgage principal, interest, and other distributions are being passed through as required, and the servicer is meeting its obligations under the terms of the offering.

Some asset-backed securities do not qualify under Regulation T as securities for whose purchase credit may be extended. They do not qualify as registered securities because none are traded on a national securities exchange. Some, particularly nonmortgage-related pass-throughs, do not qualify as OTC margin bonds because they are not corporate debt securities; the issuer is generally a servicer of the assets supporting the securities, rather than an obligor of the securities.

Rule 415

Since March 1982, when the SEC adopted Rule 415 under the Securities Act of 1933, issuers of securities could, at one time and with the same registration statement, register all securities of a particular type that were expected to be issued within a two-year period. Such registration under Rule 415 is known as shelf registration because it allows issuers to issue securities "off the shelf" in order to coincide with favorable market conditions without the delay of the registration process. Shelf registration reduces the time it takes to issue securities from several weeks to several days.[1] While their securities are on the shelf, issuers meet their disclosure requirements by referencing their periodic reports filed under the Securities Exchange Act of 1934 (e.g., 10-K and 10-Q filings).

Investment Company Act of 1940

The purpose of the Investment Company Act of 1940 is to mitigate and, to the extent possible, eliminate specific conditions that would adversely affect the national public interest and the interest of investors. Such conditions, which are enumerated in Section 1 of the 1940 Act, include lack of investor information and the selection of investment companies' portfolios that benefit their managers at the expense of their investors. The 1940 Act, therefore, requires all public investment companies to register with the SEC and to file periodic and other reports with the Commission.

The 1940 Act defines investment company as any issuer that:

• Is engaged primarily, or proposes to engage primarily, in the business of investing, reinvesting, or trading securities;

• Is engaged or proposes to engage in the business of issuing face-amount certificates of the installment type, or has been engaged in such business and has any such certificate outstanding; or

---

1 Thomas A. Pugel and Lawrence J. White, "Analysis of the Competitive Effects of Allowing Commercial Bank Affiliates to Underwrite Corporate Securities," in Ingo Walter, ed., *Deregulating Wall Street*, (New York: John Wiley & Sons, 1985).

- Is engaged or proposes to engage in the business of investing, reinvesting, owning, holding, or trading in securities, and owns or proposes to acquire investment securities having a value exceeding 40 percent of the value of such issuer's total assets (exclusive of government securities and cash items) on an unconsolidated basis.

In general, nearly all issues of asset-backed securities would involve investment companies covered by the above definition, because such securities are usually issued through limited-purpose finance companies or trusts and because receivables, mortgage loans, and mortgage-backed securities are considered securities under the 1940 Act. The 1940 Act, however, explicitly excepts 13 types of issuers from the definition of investment company. Three of these exceptions are relevant for asset-backed securities.[2]

First, the Act excepts so-called private investment companies. Issuers of securities that. have 100 or fewer beneficial owners of its securities and that does not propose to offer them publicly are not considered investment companies under the 1940 Act. When a company holds less than 10 percent of an issuer of asset-backed securities or when the total value of the issuer of asset-backed securities owned by a company is less than 10 percent of its assets, then beneficial ownership resides with one "person." If, however, a company owns more than 10 percent of an issuer of asset-backed securities, and the owned securities represent more than 10 percent of the company's assets, then the company's security holders are counted as individual beneficial owners.[3]

---

2 Glen A. Payne, "Regulatory Issues Presented by, and Available Exemptions for, Structured Financings, Under the Investment Company Act of 1940," Securities and Exchange Commission, October 26, 1987, mimeo.

3 Payne.

Small loan companies also are excepted from the definition of investment company under the 1940 Act that pertains to asset-backed securities. Any firm whose business is substantially confined to making small business loans, industrial banking, or similar businesses is excepted. SEC legal staff has stated that "similar businesses" covers businesses that engage in specialized consumer finance.[4]

The third exception, the one that is most applicable to asset-backed securities involving receivables and mortgage-related assets, is found in Section 3(c)(5) of the Act. This section excludes from the definition of investment company any firm that is not engaged in the business of issuing redeemable securities and that is primarily engaged in purchasing notes, drafts, acceptances, open accounts receivable, and other obligations representing part or all of the sales price of merchandise, insurance, and services; making loans to manufacturers, wholesalers, and retailers of, and to prospective purchasers of, specified merchandise, insurance, or services; or purchasing or otherwise acquiring mortgages and other liens on and interests on real estate. SEC staff interpretations of "other liens on and interests in real estate" indicate that the phrase includes fee interest in real estate, leasehold interest, notes fully secured by mortgages solely in real estate, whole pool agency certificates (but not private pass-through certificates), and FHLMC mortgage participation certificates. Excluded are partial pool agency certificates and residual interests from REMICs.[5]

A redeemable security, for purposes of the 1940 Act, is any security that has terms that allow the holder, upon its presentation to the issuer or to a person designated by the issuer, to receive approximately his proportionate share of the issuer's current net assets or their cash equivalent. Members of the SEC's staff have clarified this definition through interpretations.[6] They have determined that, for a security to be

4 Payne.
5 Payne.
6 Payne.

redeemable under the 1940 Act, the redeemability has to be at the holder's, rather than the issuer's, option. Also, a security that is redeemable at any time upon 30-days notice is considered to be redeemable under the 1940 Act. If a security is redeemable at the book (rather than market) value or if a security is redeemable only in the order it is received and only to the extent the issuer has liquid assets, then it is not considered a redeemable security for purposes of the 1940 Act.

As stated earlier, some issues of asset-backed securities are exempt from registration under the Investment Company Act because of the real estate exception from the definition of investment company. However, issuers not exempt under this exception may be covered by the exemption provided for under Section 6(c). This section authorizes the SEC to conditionally or unconditionally exempt any person, security, or transaction from any provision of the 1940 Act to the extent necessary, appropriate, and consistent with the protection of investors and the purposes fairly intended by the 1940 Act. Such exemptions are granted on a case-by-case basis, and (except in emergency situations) the SEC must publish notice of an exemption before granting it.

Collateralized Mortgage Obligations

CMOs that are not collateralized by whole pool agency certificates or by whole mortgage loans do not qualify for the Section 3(c)(5) exemption and, therefore, must seek for exemption from the requirements of the 1940 Act under Section 6(c).[7] Issuers of CMOs, which are collateralized by partial pool agency certificates or notes secured by mortgage loans and mortgage collateral have been granted exemptions from all or some of the 1940's Act's requirements.[8]

---

7 REMICs are afforded similar treatment as CMOs under the Investment Company Act of 1940 by the Securities and Exchange Commission.
8 Payne.

The requirements of registering under the 1940 Act, which entail, for example, prohibitions on multiple classes of securities, limitations on sales and distribution, and restrictions on transactions involving affiliated persons, are considered to be so expensive and restrictive that most issues of asset-backed securities "could not, as a practical matter, operate under the 1940 Act."[9] Consequently, most issues of asset-backed securities that have been sold have been exempted from the Act.

State Blue Sky Laws

In addition to federal securities laws, individual states have laws of their own that also require registration of securities. Most such state laws exempt securities that are senior to, or of equal rank with securities of the same issuer that are listed on a national securities exchange or specified regional exchanges. For example, the Uniform Securities Act, which has been approved by nearly every state, provides for such an exemption.[10] The state securities regulators, which have considered whether asset-backed securities should be exempted, have been of the opinion that they should not be exempt because asset-backed securities are not obligations of the originator.

A Bill to Improve the Marketability of Asset-Backed Securities

In early 1988, a member of the Senate Banking Subcommittee on Securities introduced legislation to improve the marketability of certain nonmortgage-related asset-backed securities. The bill, entitled the "Receivable-Related Securities Market Improvement Act of 1988," was patterned somewhat after the Secondary Mortgage Market Enhancement Act of 1984

---

9 Payne.

10 *Congressional Record—Senate*, February 1, 1988, S375.

but concerned securities backed by loans other than residential mortgage loans, including agricultural loans, loans to lesser developed countries, small business loans, automobile loans, trade receivables, and student loans. The proposed Act attempts to reduce the disclosure requirements, increase the number of potential investors, and facilitate the structuring of asset-backed securities by specifically addressing provisions of the Securities Act of 1933 and the Securities Exchange Act of 1934, Rule 415, state legal investment statutes, state Blue Sky laws, and the Federal Reserve Board's treatment of asset sales with recourse with respect to reserve requirements.

The proposed legislation would lessen the registration and disclosure requirements for some nonmortgage-related asset-backed securities by extending the exemption for mortgage-backed securities sold to sophisticated investors (under the terms in the 1933 Act) to receivable-related securities. "Receivable-related security" would be defined as an investment grade security that is secured by a motor vehicle loan or lease, export financing or trade receivable, small business loan, an education loan, agricultural loan, or loan to a sovereign loan to a lesser developed country.[11] The security should represent ownership of one or more promissory notes or certificates of interest in such notes, which are directly secured by a lien and were originated by a savings and loan association, a bank, credit union, insurance company, or similar organization that is supervised by a state or federal authority.

The proposed act would also reduce the information cost associated with issuing asset-backed securities by allowing receivable-related pass-through securities to qualify for shelf-registration and by preempting state Blue Sky laws to provide that certain receivable-related securities be exempt from state registration. Any receivable-related securities exempt under the 1933 Act, as amended by the proposed Act, would be exempt from state registration to the same extent as any obliga-

---

11 Glaring, albeit intentional, omissions to the definition were credit card receivables and other consumer debt.

tion issued by or guaranteed by the United States or an agency of the United States. The proposed Act would give the individual states seven years to enact legislation to override this provision.

The proposed Act also attempts to increase the number of potential purchasers of certain asset-backed securities. It would amend the definition of margin bond in Regulation T of the Federal Reserve Board to include certain asset-backed securities, not exempt under the 1933 and 1934 Acts, under conditions similar to those that are required for mortgage pass-through securities to qualify as margin bonds. The proposed act would also preempt certain state legal investment statutes that govern the types of assets in which state-regulated or state chartered organizations (such as banks, savings and loans associations, employee pension funds, and insurance companies) can invest.[12] While these laws vary from state to state, few states have expressly authorized the investment in asset-backed securities. In some states, organizations find the authority to invest in asset-backed securities in provisions that allow for investments in the receivables themselves; in other states, state-chartered entities cannot invest in certain asset-backed securities at all. The proposed law would preempt state laws so that certain investment-grade asset-backed securities would be given the same treatment as federal government securities. Again, the individual states would be given seven years to enact legislation that would negate this preemption.

In addition to reducing the information costs and increasing the number of potential purchasers of asset-backed securities, the proposed legislation also seeks to facilitate the structuring of such securities by exempting the sale of receivables with recourse, when the recourse amounts to 10 percent or less of the dollar amount sold from the definition of deposit under the Federal Reserve Board's Regulation D. As discussed in chapter 7, such a provision would extend the 10-percent rule now applied to residential mortgages to other receivables.

12 *Congressional Record-Senate*, February 1, 1988, S375.

The proposed Receivable-Related Securities Act did not become law in 1988, but may be resurrected, perhaps in a slightly different form, in 1989.

CHAPTER 9

The Authority of
▶ Commercial Banks ◀
to Underwrite
Asset-Backed Securities

COMMERCIAL BANKS originate and hold a substantial portion of the types of assets that are currently securitized. They have issued nearly one-third of the publicly offered nonmortgage-related asset-backed securities. Underwriting such securities, especially their own issues, therefore, seems to be a logical extension of their current activities. Yet, the authority of commercial banks or their affiliates to "underwrite" or "deal in" asset-backed securities is not unambiguous.

This chapter briefly discusses the laws that govern the permissibility of commercial banks to underwrite asset-backed securities and the interpretations of these laws by the Federal Reserve Board, the Office of the Comptroller of the Currency, and the securities industry. The underwriting of asset-backed securities by commercial banks and their affiliates to date is also discussed.

Laws Concerning Banks' Underwriting Powers

Prior to the 1930s, it was common for investment banking and commercial banking activities to be carried out within the same financial institution. The alleged abuses uncovered by the Senate investigation of the banking collapse of the 1930s, however, aroused great public indignation and proved instrumental in gaining passage of the Banking Act of 1933.[1] The Act, commonly known as the Glass-Steagall Act, (from the names of the chairmen of the Senate and House banking committees), contains provisions that affected nearly every aspect of banking, including those that separate commercial banking and investment banking. This Act, along with the Bank Holding Company Act and the National Bank Act, forms the basis for the debate about the authority of banks to underwrite and deal in asset-backed securities.

The Glass-Steagall Act

Sections 5(c), 16, 20, 21 and 32 of the Glass-Steagall Act, separate commercial and investment banking.

Section 16 prohibits national banks from underwriting any issue of securities or stock and restricts their dealing in securities to purchasing and selling securities and stock without recourse, "solely upon the order, and for the account of, customers, and in no case for [their] own account[s]." Section 16, however, does not apply to U.S. Treasury securities and municipal general obligation bonds. Section 5(c) extends the restrictions in Section 16 to state banks that are members of the Federal Reserve System.

Section 20 prohibits member banks from affiliating with any organization that is "engaged principally in the issue, flotation, underwriting, public sale, or distribution at wholesale or

---

1 George G. Kaufman and Larry R. Mote, "Securities Activities of Commercial Banks: The Current Economic and Legal Environment," *Staff Memoranda*, Federal Reserve Bank of Chicago, 88–4 (1988).

retail or through syndicate participation of stocks, bonds, debentures, notes, or other securities." And, according to Section 21, such an organization cannot "engage at the same time to any extent whatever in the business of receiving deposits."

Section 32 prohibits any officer, director, or employee of such an organization from serving at "the same time as an officer, director, or employee of any member bank."

The Bank Holding Company Act

In addition to the Glass-Steagall Act, the permissibility of securities underwriting by affiliates of commercial banks is governed by the Bank Holding Company Act of 1956 and its amendments of 1970. Section 4(c)(8) of the Bank Holding Company Act defines and regulates all nonbank activities of bank holding companies. It is the Federal Reserve Board's responsibility to determine which activities are permissible under the Bank Holding Company Act. For the Fed either by regulation or by order, to deem a new activity permissible the activity must be proven to be "so closely related to banking or managing or controlling banks as to be a proper incident thereto." That is, it must pass the "closely related" and the "proper incident" (public benefits) tests.

In finding an activity to be "closely related" to banking, the Fed considers whether: (1) banks engage in the proposed activity; (2) banks generally provide services that are operationally or functionally so similar to the proposed activity as to equip them particularly well to engage in the proposed activity; or (3) banks generally provide services that are so integrally related to the proposed activity as to require their provision in a specialized form.

Using the "proper incident" test, the Fed considers whether or not the performance of the activity by the bank holding company can reasonably be expected to produce benefits to the public. The Fed looks for benefits such as greater convenience, increased competition, and gains in efficiency that outweigh possible adverse effects, such as undue concentration of resources, decreased or unfair competition, conflicts of interest, and unsound banking practices.

The National Bank Act

A third statute that bears on the underwriting authority of commercial banks is the National Bank Act of 1864 and its amendments. This Act gives national banks the authority to conduct enumerated banking activities. For example, the National Bank Act expressly gives national banks the authority (1) to accept general deposits (but not collateralized deposits), (2) to lend money on personal security and to make loans secured by real estate, and (3) "to discount and negotiate promissory notes, drafts, bills of exchange, and other evidences of debt."

The National Bank Act also contains an "incidental powers" clause, which allows for changes in the methods of conducting lawful bank activities. The incidental powers clause gives national banks "all such incidental powers as shall be necessary to carry out the business of banking."

Because "the business of banking" is not defined in the National Bank Act, this phrase has been the subject of much litigation. Perhaps the most famous case that involved the incidental powers clause was the 1972 case of *Arnold Tours, Inc. v. Camp.*[2] The incidental power in question was travel agency but the major outcome of the case was not the decision as to whether or not banks could act as travel agents, but the rather restrictive interpretation of the incidental powers clause by the Court of Appeals. The Court stated that an activity is authorized "if it is convenient or useful in connection with the performance of one of the bank's established activities pursuant to its expressed powers under the National Bank Act. If this connection . . . does not exist, the activity is not authorized as an incidental power." Examples of lawful incidental powers include the leasing of personal property and the issuance of letters of credit.

---

2 Arnold Tours, Inc. v. Camp, 472 F.2d 427,432 (1st Cir. 1972)

Interpretations and Opinions

The laws discussed above are open to much interpretation. Experience has shown that the language of the Glass-Steagall Act—in particular, the terms "principally engaged" and "primarily engaged"—lends itself to a variety of interpretations. Similarly, the terms "closely related to banking" and "proper incident thereto" in the Bank Holding Company Act have been the subject of much interpretation. And as mentioned above, the phrase "business of banking" in the incidental powers clause of the National Bank Act is not defined.

The Federal Reserve Board, the Office of the Comptroller of the Currency (OCC), and the securities industry that have interpreted these statutes and rendered opinions on the permissibility of underwriting and dealing in asset-backed securities by commercial banks and their affiliates. The securities industry has interpreted the relevant statutes in such a way as to conclude that banks and their affiliates are not permitted to underwrite any asset-backed securities. The OCC, the primary regulator of national banks, has looked primarily to the National Bank Act and the Glass-Steagall Act in determining that underwriting asset-backed securities is a permissible activity for commercial banks, while the Fed, the primary regulator of bank holding companies, has looked to the Glass-Steagall Act and the Bank Holding Company Act in concluding that underwriting asset-backed securities is permissible for affiliates of commercial banks.

The Comptroller of the Currency

The Office of the Comptroller of the Currency is of the opinion that "the initial placement of [a bank's] own" asset-backed securities is authorized under the national banking laws and does not violate the Glass-Steagall Act.[3] The primary basis for

---

3 The OCC does not consider the distribution of a bank's own securities "underwriting" because the bank does not purchase and resell them.

the OCC's opinion is found in a June 1987 letter to Russell A. Freeman, Esquire, in response to Freeman's earlier request for a copy of the OCC's response to an inquiry from the Securities Industry Association regarding the permissibility of Security Pacific National Bank's plan to sell its own mortgage pass-through certificates. Although the securities in question were mortgage-related, the Comptroller made clear that his opinion also applies to other types of asset-backed securities.

The Comptroller's opinion is based primarily on three points. First, the authority of a bank to sell its assets is granted by the national banking laws. Second, the form of the sale does not matter. Third, the Glass-Steagall Act is not violated, because asset-backed securities are not securities for purposes of the Glass-Steagall Act and because the "initial placement" of a bank's own securities does not constitute "underwriting " or "dealing."

As pointed out in the Comptroller's June 1987 letter, the sale of a bank's assets "is fully permitted under the national banking laws." Furthermore, mortgage pass-throughs represent "nothing more than the negotiation of evidences of debt and the sale of real estate loans, which is expressly authorized under [the National Bank Act]."

According to the Comptroller, the fact that a sale of assets is accomplished with certificates, "an activity which [the OCC] long has approved, does not alter in any respect the substance of the transaction, nor its permissibility under the national banking laws." According to the Comptroller, even if the most restrictive test of incidental powers *(Arnold Tours, Inc.)* is applied, "the process of pooling bank assets and selling certificates representing interests therein can be 'convenient or useful' to a bank's ability to sell its assets."

As to the violation of the Glass-Steagall Act's prohibition on underwriting by commercial banks, the Comptroller stated that Glass-Steagall is not implicated because pass-throughs are not securities for purposes of the Act "because certificate-holders have essentially the same rights, liabilities, and risks as if they were the owners of the underlying assets, and the certificates are considered to be substantially the same as those assets."[4] But even if pass-through certificates were securities, the OCC does not consider Security Pacific's program to be "underwriting" or "dealing." Mere participation by a bank in the initial placement of its own securities with investors without the subsequent repurchase of those securities does not involve the "business of underwriting" nor does it involve the "business of dealing."

The Federal Reserve Board

In response to a series of applications filed by three large bank holding companies during the first half of 1987, the Federal Reserve Board ruled that underwriting and dealing in mortgage-backed securities, as well as commercial paper and municipal revenue bonds, are permissible under the Bank Holding Company Act and do not violate the Glass Steagall Act so long as a subsidiary's underwriting or dealing in such securities is insubstantial.[5] In July 1987 the Fed ruled that securities backed by consumer-related receivables, such as auto loans and credit card accounts, were to be afforded the same treatment as commercial paper, municipal revenue bonds, and mortgage-backed securities.

While the Fed and the Comptroller generally agree that "underwriting" asset-backed securities is a permissible activity for banking firms, they arrived at their decisions somewhat differently. The Fed's decision was a response to the applications of bank holding companies to engage (through wholly-owned nonbank subsidiaries) in underwriting and dealing in mortgage-backed and other asset-backed securities as well as

---

4 The Comptroller also is of the opinion that national banks are authorized to underwrite collateralized mortgage obligation bonds. See Robert L. Clarke, Comptroller of the Currency, letter to the Honorable Alfonse M. D'Amato, Chairman, Subcommittee on Securities, Committee on Banking, Housing and Urban Affairs, United States Senate, June 18, 1986.

5 Citicorp, J.P. Morgan & Co. Inc., and Bankers Trust New York Corp. *Federal Reserve Bulletin* (June 1987).

municipal revenue bonds and commercial paper. The Bank Holding Company Act, which governs the permissibility of nonbank activities for bank holding companies, therefore, was implicated. Unlike the Comptroller, however, the Fed also implicated the Glass-Steagall Act.

The three bank holding companies proposed to add un-underwriting and dealing in asset-backed securities, municipal revenue bonds, and commercial paper to the activities of existing subsidiaries, that at the time engaged in underwriting government securities and general obligation municipal bonds. According to the Fed, mortgage-backed securities and securities backed by consumer receivables, as well as municipal revenue bonds and commercial paper, are "ineligible" securities for purposes of the Glass-Steagall Act. It should be noted that the OCC disagreed with the Fed's characterization of these securities as "ineligible." The OCC held that banks may underwrite and deal in "mortgage-related and consumer receivables-related obligations . . . under the national banking laws."[6]

In determining whether the proposal would violate Glass-Steagall, the Board had to determine whether underwriting "eligible" securities pursuant to Section 16 of the Glass-Steagall Act, which concerns the activities of member banks, should be considered a permissible activity for the purposes of applying Section 20, which concerns the activities of affiliates of member banks, to the proposed underwriting subsidiaries. The Board also had to determine whether the subsidiaries would be "engaged principally" in underwriting according to Section 20 of the Glass-Steagall Act.

On the first point, the Board concluded that securities "eligible" for purposes of Section 16 should also be eligible under Section 20. The Board noted that the Supreme Court has stated that Congress did not intend to impose a less stringent standard on member bank affiliates under Section 20 than that

6 Dean S. Marriott, Senior Deputy Comptroller for Bank Supervision, letter to Mr. William W. Wiles, Secretary, January 30, 1987.

it applied to member banks under Section 16. Therefore, the Board had previously authorized bank holding companies to underwrite and deal in "eligible" securities under Section 16 of the Glass-Steagall Act.[7]

On the second point, the Board concluded that the term "engaged principally" would allow the underwriting of asset-backed securities to be conducted by an affiliate of a member bank if it were relatively "insubstantial" relative to the total activity of the affiliate and the size of the market for asset-backed securities. The Board, in a previous case, defined "insubstantial" to be 5 percent or less of the affiliate's total gross revenues and 5 percent or less of the domestic market for such securities.[8]

With respect to the Glass-Steagall Act, the securities industry held that the term "securities" in Section 20 encompasses all securities, not just those ineligible pursuant to Section 16.[9] Therefore, the industry held that "engaged principally" in Section 20 should apply to underwriting all securities, and because the underwriting subsidiaries of bank holding companies would be involved solely in underwriting, their activities would violate Glass-Steagall.[10]

Furthermore, the securities industry argued that the term "principally" must be interpreted "to denote any substantial, significant, regular or nonincidental activity, whether or not it is the largest activity of the affiliate."[11]

---

7 See, for example, United Bancorp, *Federal Reserve Bulletin* (March 1978).

8 Bankers Trust New York Corporation, *Federal Reserve Bulletin* (February 1987.)

9 The protestants of the securities industry primarily included the Securities Industry Association, a trade association of investment banks, and the Investment Company Institute, a trade group of the mutual fund industry.

10 Charirman Volcker and Governor Angell of the Federal Reserve Board were also of this opinion. See *Federal Reserve Bulletin* (June 1987), pp. 505-506.

11 *Federal Reserve Bulletin* (June 1987), p. 478.

In addition to determining that underwriting asset-backed securities did not violate the Glass-Steagall Act, the Fed also had to apply the "closely related" and "public benefits" tests of the Bank Holding Company Act to the proposed activity. The Fed concluded that the proposed activities are a natural extension of activities currently conducted by banks, involving little additional risk or new conflicts of interest. Furthermore, the Fed noted that such activities had the potential to yield significant public benefits in the form of increased competition and convenience and lower costs.

With respect to the Bank Holding Company Act and whether underwriting asset-backed securities is closely related to banking, the securities industry argued that there is a major difference between underwriting activities permitted member banks and the underwriting of the proposed ineligible securities. That is, eligible securities are generally offered to dealers through competitive bidding arrangements, while revenue bonds and asset-backed securities are usually negotiated. The Fed, however, held that bank participation in underwriting and dealing in eligible securities has made them "sufficiently familiar with negotiating processes as well as . . . competitive bidding."[12]

The securities industry also did not agree with the Fed that securities underwriting is a "proper incident" to banking. The securities industry indicated that there are potential conflicts of interest

> caused by the underwriting subsidiaries' 'salesman's stake' and promotional incentives in the securities it underwrites or deals in, loss of public confidence in the bank if the affiliate experiences losses on its securities activities, risk to the bank holding company as a result of possible underwriting losses by the affiliate's, undue concentration of resources resulting from greater domination of financial

---

12 *Federal Reserve Bulletin* (June 1987), p. 488.

markets by banking organizations, and unfair competition, such as the affiliate obtaining funding from low-cost bank deposits or gaining access to confidential customer information held by the bank.[13]

While the Fed held that these conflicts are not likely to occur, it did take note of some potential adverse effects and conflicts of interest from the proposed underwriting activities and, therefore, did place limitations on the underwriting of asset-backed securities (see Figure 9-1). For example, under-writing subsidiaries cannot share offices or personnel with affiliate banks.

Figure 9-1 Overview of Limitations Imposed by the Fed on Underwriting Subsidiaries of Bank Holding Companies

- The underwriting activities of underwriting subsidiaries will not be conducted by affilitate banks or by the banks' personnel.

- The underwriting subsidiaries and their affiliate banks may not have common officers, directors, or employees.

- Affiliate banks may not act as agents or engage in marketing activities for the underwriting subsidiaries.

- The underwriting subsidiaries and their affiliate banks should have separate offices.

- Each underwriting subsidiaries must disclose to each of its customers the difference between the underwriting subsidiary and its affiliate banks, pointing out that its obligations are not obligations of an affiliate bank.

- Each underwriting subsidiary must disclose any material lending relationship between the issuer of securities it is underwriting and a bank or lending affiliate.

- Limitations are placed on the type of ineligible securities that underwriting subsidiaries may underwrite and deal in.

- Limitations are placed on credit extensions of affiliates in relation to the activities of underwriting subsidiaries.

13 *Federal Reserve Bulletin* (June 1987), p. 491.

Also, underwriting subsidiaries are subject to a number of disclosure requirements. The Board requires that each underwriting subsidiary disclose the difference between the underwriting subsidiary and its banking affiliates to its customers and point out that the obligations of the subsidiary are not the obligations of any banking affiliates. The underwriting subsidiary should also disclose any material lending relationship between the issuer and a bank or lending affiliate of the subsidiary.

To guard against unsound banking practices, the Board also placed restrictions on the extension of credit by affiliates of underwriting subsidiaries in connection with ineligible securities underwritten by the subsidiaries (see Figure 9-2).

Figure 9-2   Limitations on the Extension of Credit by Affiliates of Underwriting Subsidiaries

- Affiliate banks may not extend credit to customers that are secured by any ineligible security underwritten by an underwriting subsidiary or for the purpose of purchasing securities from the underwriting subsidiaries during the course of underwritings.

- No affiliate may make loans to issuers of ineligible securities underwritten by the underwriting subsidiaries for the purpose of payment of principal and interest on such securities.

- No affiliate may enter into a standby letter of credit, asset purchase agreement, indemnity, insurance, or other facility that might be viewed as enhancing the creditworthiness or marketability of ineligible securities underwritten by an underwriting subsidiary.

- No affilitate should purchase, as principal, ineligible securities underwritten by an underwriting subsidiary during the underwriting period and for 60 days thereafter.

- No affilitate should purchase from an underwriting subsidiary any ineligible security in which the underwriting subsidiary makes a market.

Any lending affiliate of an underwriting subsidary may not extend to a customer credit that "is secured by, or for the purpose of purchasing, any ineligible security that the subsidiary un-derwrites during the course of the underwriting or for the purpose of purchasing from the subsidiary any ineligible security in which the underwriting subsidiary makes a market."[14] In addition, neither the bank holding companies nor any of their subsidiaries are permitted to make loans to an issuer of ineligible securities underwritten by the underwriting subsidiaries for the purpose of paying principal or interest on such securities, and the bank holding company and its subsidiaries may not provide a standby letter of credit or other form of credit enhancement for the ineligible securities underwritten by the underwriting subsidiary.

Underwriting subsidiaries can underwrite and deal only in certain types of ineligible securities (see Figure 9-3). They may underwrite only securities backed by consumer-related receivables that are investment grade and mortgage securities that are secured by or represent interests in one-to-four-family residential mortgage loans that are rated as investment-quality. Perhaps the most important restriction on the type of ineligible securities is one that prohibits underwriting subsidiaries from underwriting and dealing in their affiliates' own issues of asset-backed securities. This restriction implies that such securities will be underwritten by nonaffiliated firms or by a subsidiary of a bank affiliate, as this is permitted by the OCC.

Current Events

As discussed above, the securities industry does not agree with the Comptroller's or the Fed's opinions that it is permissible for banking firms to underwrite asset-backed securities. Consequently, the Securities Industry Association (SIA) challenged the Fed's orders in court, and the underwriting subsidiaries of

---

14 " *Federal Reserve Bulletin* (June 1987), p. 496.

208   The Environment for Asset-Backed Securities

Figure 9-3   Limitations on Types of Ineligible Securities that Underwriting Subsidiaries Can Underwrite or Deal In

- Underwriting subsidiaries may not underwrite or deal in any ineligible securities issued by its affiliates or representing interests in, or secured by, obligations originated or sponsored by its affilitates (except for grantor trusts or special-purpose corporations created to facilitate the underwriting of securities backed by loans originated by a nonaffiliated lender).

- Underwriting subsidiaries are limited to underwriting and dealing in investment-grade mortgage securities that are secured by or represent interests in one-to-four-family residential mortgage loans.

- Underwriting subsidiaries are limited to underwriting and dealing in investment-grade securities that are secured by or represent interests in consumer-related receivables.

bank holding companies were ·prevented from immediately taking advantage of their new powers.[15] The law suit resulted in a stay on the new powers. The Fed's ruling was eventually upheld by a federal appeals court in February 1988, and the following June, the U.S. Supreme Court refused to review the lower court's decision. Even without the SIA's suit, however, implementation of the new powers would have been delayed. The Competitive Equality Banking Act of 1987 placed a moratorium on the exercise of new nonbank powers, including securities underwriting activities, by bank holding companies until March 1, 1988.

---

15 By June 1988, the Federal Reserve Board had approved the applications of nine more bank holding companies to establish underwriting subsidiaries: Chemical New York Corp.; Chase Manhattan, Manufacturers Hanover, Security Pacific, PNC Financial, Marine Midland Banks, First Interstate, Bank of New England, and Bank of Montreal.

Similarly, the Securities Industry Association sued the OCC after it authorized Security Pacific to issue and sell its own mortgage-backed securities in June 1987. The SIA contends that the Glass-Steagall Act is violated. At the end of December 1988, a U.S. District Court ruled that national banks cannot underwrite securities backed by their own assets. The OCC and Security Pacific are expected to appeal the ruling.

Since the June 1987 letter, several other banks have underwritten their own asset-backed securities. All bank-underwritten issues other than Security Pacific's mortgage pass-throughs, however, have been co-managed by the issuing commercial banks and an investment bank. The SIA has not filed suit in these instances.

PART IV

▶ Some Conclusions ◀

CHAPTER 10
▶ Implications of ◀ Securitization

IN 1985, when the securitization of nonmortgage-related assets was still in its infancy, it was viewed by some as a fad and by others as the means by which the entire financial services industry would be transformed.[1] Three years later, the infant has become a toddler whose growth by most measures has not been as phenomenal as some had predicted but has, nevertheless, been impressive.[2] This chapter first reviews the overall growth and development of the market for nonmortgage asset-backed securities relative to that for mortgage securities. Second, it discusses the likely impact that trends and changes in the financial services industry and in the economy will have on the future of securitization. Third, it examines the impact that securitization has had and will likely have on the financial services industry.

---

1 James McCormick, "Transforming Banks into Capital-Efficient Intermediaries: Part I," *American Banker*, September 20, 1985.

2 See Harvey D. Shapiro, "The Securitization of Practically Everything," *Institutional Investor* (May 1985).

From Infant to Toddler

Early in 1985, the first nonmortgage-related issues of asset-backed securities were sold publicly. Sperry issued nearly $200 million in notes backed by computer leases, and Valley National Bank and Marine Midland Bank each originated pass-through certificates backed by automobile loans. By year-end, roughly $1.2 billion of securities backed by nonmortgage-related assets had been issued. At that time, some market observers predicted that the market for such securities would grow to the size of the market for mortgage-backed securities, which then consisted of more than $400 billion in mortgage securities outstanding and over $100 billion of new securities issued.[3]

Three years later, nearly $30 billion of nonmortgage-related asset-backed securities had been issued publicly, and annual issuance was at about $10 to 12 billion. Obviously, the size of this market is nowhere near that of the mortgage securities market, even when one considers that the size of the private placement market for asset-backed securities is about equal to the public market. Such a comparison, however, is akin to comparing a pre-schooler with a high school senior; the market for mortgage-backed securities is about 14 years older than the market for other types of asset-backed securities.

As shown in Figure 10-1, when the market for mortgage securities is compared with its non-mortgage counterpart at similar points in their development, the issuance of non-mortgage-related asset-backed securities seems strong. In the first three years of their existence, less than $6 billion of mortgage securities were issued. If this dollar amount is adjusted for inflation and put in 1987-equivalent dollars, then roughly $16 billion were issued. Furthermore, a market observer in 1973, when mortgage securities were only three years old, would have seen annual issuance of mortgage securities at about $3 billion annually, or $7.5 billion in 1987 dollars.

---

3 Federal Home Loan Mortgage Corporation.

Figure 10-1

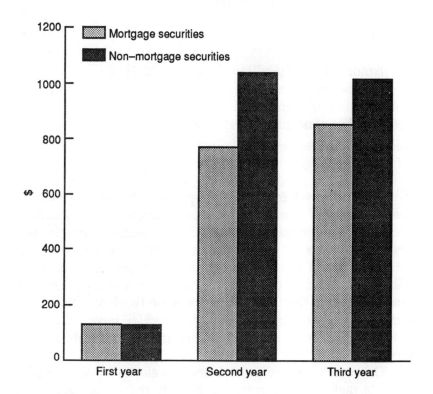

Table 10-1   Public Offerings of Nonmortgage-Related
Asset-Backed Securities

	1985	1986	1987	*Through* *June 1988*
Amount issued ($billions)	$1.2	$10.0	$10.2	$6.0
Number of issues	7	16	37	22
Types of collateral	2	2	9	7
Number of originator/issuers	6	9	25	19

Source: *Asset Sales Report*, various issues.

When viewed from this perspective the development of the market for nonmortgage-related asset-backed securities seems fairly impressive. And when one considers that, in their first few years of existence, the only mortgage-backed securities issued were those of the federal mortgage agencies (Ginnie Mae and Freddie Mac), which carry a U.S. government guarantee, and that over 90 percent of the loans that were securitized were also guaranteed by the U.S. government, the first three years of nonmortgage-related securitization seem *very* impressive.

Other measures of growth and development also seem to indicate that asset securitization is more than a fad (see Table 10-1). The yearly issuance of publicly offered nonmortgage-related asset-backed securities has increased over fivefold, from seven issues in 1985 to 37 in 1987. In the first half of 1988, 22 issues were sold publicly. The types of collateral that back public issues of asset-backed securities have increased from two (auto loans and computer leases) in 1985 to nine in 1987 (see Figure 10-2). By June 1988, 10 types of assets had backed public offerings of nonmortgage asset-backed securities, and several other types had backed private issues. Furthermore, the number of originators/issuers of publicly offered asset-backed securities was 38 as of June 1988; 15 of these were repeat issuers; and two sold securities backed by auto loans as well as securities backed by credit card receivables.

Figure 10-2 History of the Types of Nonmortgage-Related Assets Securitized (and Sold through Public Offerings)

1985	1986	1987	Through June 1988
Computer leases	Computer leases	Auto loans	Auto loans
Auto loans	Auto loans	Credit cards	Credit cards
		Mack truck loans	Mack truck loans
		Manufactured home loans	Manufactured home loans
		Trade receivables	
		Junk bonds	
		Equipment notes	
		Auto leases	
		Unsecured consumer loans	

Source: *Asset Sales Report,* various issues.

With the entry of more asset-backed securities issuers, especially those that repeatedly go to the market, the volume of nonmortgage-related asset-backed securities should continue to grow. Nonmortgage-related asset-backed securities may never rival mortgage-backed securities, however. The size of the primary market for mortgage loans is almost five times larger than the market for consumer debt, which currently is the most frequently securitized type of nonmortgage asset.

In addition, it is unlikely that all loans will be securitized. As discussed in chapter 1, all loans are not as cheaply securitized as others. Even within the category of residential mortgage loans, some loans—mainly, those that do not conform to the criteria of the federal mortgage agencies—are more difficult to securitize than others. Consequently, some mortgages remain on the books of their originators or their purchasers as whole loans. Similarly, not all auto loans and credit card receivables are likely to be securitized for one reason or another, and some types of loans will probably never be securitized. It is, however, highly likely that the process of securitization will coexist along with more traditional methods of funding, and securitized assets will be held in portfolios along with whole loans and other assets.

The Effect of Economic and Industry Trends

The market for nonmortgage asset-backed securities is likely to thrive as asset securitization remains an important means by which commercial banks and savings and loan associations, as well as nonfinancial firms, manage interest-rate risk, enhance the liquidity and increase the diversification of their portfolios, fund new assets and operations, and reduce their regulatory tax burden. Developments in the financial services industry and in the economy will affect whether or not securitization is the most cost-effective means to achieve these ends. In the near term, changes in commercial bank capital regulations and generally accepted accounting principles, as well as the increasing occurrence of corporate takeovers and product line and geographic expansion by banking firms, are likely to have a significant impact on securitization.

Risk-Based Capital

Regulatory taxes are the most often cited motivation for securitization.[4] As discussed in Chapter 7, securitization may

4 See, for example, Mark Flannery, "Deposit Insurance, Capital Regulation and the Choice of Bank Loan Default Rates, " University of North Carolina, 1987, Mimeo; Stuart I. Greenbaum and Anjan V. Thakor, "Bank Funding Modes: Securitization versus Deposits," *Journal of Banking and Finance* (September 1987); Christine Pavel and David Phillis "Why Commercial Banks Sell Loans, An Empirical Analysis," *Economic Perspectives*, Federal Reserve Bank of Chicago (May/June 1987).

allow a depository institution to avoid deposit insurance premiums and reserve and capital requirements. One reason that commercial banks sell assets, either as whole loans, participations, or pass-through certificates, is that regulatory taxes make funding the underlying assets an unprofitable venture.[5]

Capital requirements account for the largest percentage of the total regulatory tax bill.[6] The current proposal for risk-based capital guidelines, therefore, should significantly influence asset securitization.

Since early 1987, the Federal Reserve System, the Federal Deposit Insurance Corporation, and the Office of the Comptroller of the Currency have been moving the commercial banking industry toward a system of risk-based capital. At that time, the Fed proposed guidelines that prescribed minimum levels of bank capital as a weighted percentage of assets; the weights were assigned according to the perceived credit risks of the assets. In late 1987, the Basle Committee of the Bank for International Settlements (BIS) developed guidelines for risk-based capital that were designed to be internationally consistent.[7] The proposal specified weights for various assets and for off-balance-sheet items such as standby letters of credit and loan commitments. It also allows for a gradual transition from the current capital guidelines, which do not account for the different levels of risk among types of assets, do not include off-balance-sheet items, and are not consistent among countries. The proposal calls for the guidelines to be fully implemented by 1992.

In response to the BIS framework, the Fed revised its earlier proposal. According to the revised proposal, cash and cash equivalents are assigned a weight of zero (i.e., no minimum

5 Chapter 1 and 7 discuss the impact of regulatory taxes on profitability.

6 Herbert Baer and Christine Pavel, "Does Regulation Drive Innovation?" *Economic Perspectives*, Federal Reserve Bank of Chicago, (March/April 1988).

7 The Basle Committee consists of central bankers and supervisory authorities from Belgium, Canada, France, Germany, Italy Japan, Netherlands, Sweden, Switzerland, the United Kingdom, the United States and Luxembourg.

capital is required for these types of assets). Certain bank and governmental claims are assigned weights of 10 or 20 percent. FHA and VA mortgage loans are weighted at 10 percent because they are guaranteed by an agency of the U.S. goverment. One-to-four-family conventional mortgage loans are weighted at 50 percent if their loan-to-value ratios are 80 percent or less, while all other mortgage loans have 100 percent weights. Other claims on the private sector (e.g., commmercial loans and consumer loans) also are weighted at 100 percent.

In addition, off-balance-sheet items are included in the calculation of total risk-adjusted assets. The two off-balance-sheet items that are most likely to affect the issuance of asset-backed securities are direct financial guarantees, such as letters of credit, and sales of assets with recourse. Letters of credit that serve as financial guarantees for loans and securities will carry weights of 100 percent under the BIS and revised Federal Reserve guidelines. Asset sales with recourse will be weighted according to the on-balance-sheet weights of the assets sold.

Foreign banks, as noted in chapter 2, are the largest providers of letters of credit that support issues of asset-backed securities. The BIS capital guidelines will apply to these foreign banks, which, therefore, will be required to hold a certain amount of capital against financial guarantees. Currently, they are not required to hold any capital against these off-balance-sheet items. The prices of financial guarantees, therefore, will likely increase, perhaps making some marginally profitable securitization deals unprofitable.

To the extent that the new risk-based capital guidelines bring capital requirements into line with the levels that the market would require in the absence of regulation and deposit insurance, incentives to securitized assets should be decreased. The proposed risk-based guidelines, however, do not go far enough in this regard. Most assets that are securitized are weighted at 100 percent. So the new guidelines would not decrease the amount of capital that a bank must hold against these assets, and they would not give banks an incentive to fund these assets themselves; rather, the actual impact will be to increase capital that would be held against them. Because the required percentage of capital to be applied to risk-adjusted assets will increase from six percent to eight percent, the marginal capital ratio for assets weighted at 100 percent will likewise increase from six percent to eight percent.[8] Even the mortgage loans that would qualify for 50-percent weighting will probably still be securitized because they usually can be swapped for federal agency securities, which carry a weight of 20 percent.[9]

Since most in the financial services industry believe that risk-based capital guidelines will be implemented, banks have been preparing for them to be phased in. Some banks have more preparing to do than others. Large banks are usually more thinly capitalized than small banks, and large banks usually have more off-balance-sheet items than small banks. Therefore, large banks are more likely than smaller organizations to be capital deficient under a risk-based capital regime. This situation should have a positive influence on the asset-backed securities markets. Large banking firms have been the primary securitizers of assets, and they have the largest holdings of readily securitizable assets, such as auto loans, credit card receivables, and mortgage loans.

Table 10-2, lists 20 large banking organizations that would not have been adequately capitalized if the proposed risk-based guidelines had been fully in place at the end of March 1988. Altogether, these 20 banking firms will need to raise nearly $9 billion of capital. Rather than go to the equity markets, they could sell or securitize assets. About half of the firms in Table 10-2 are already experienced in securitizing non-mortgage assets, and over half are among the largest sellers of commercial loans.

8 Under the proposed guidelines, core capital (essentially, common equity and retained earnings) will have to equal four percent of adjusted assets by 1992. The remaining four percent can consist of subordinated debt and loan loss reserves.

9 FNMAs and FHLMC PCs and securities backed by these government-sponsored agencies will be weighted at 20 percent.

Table 10-2 The Most Capital-Deficient Bank Holdings Companies (March 1988)

	Capital Ratio	Total Shortfall under 1992 Rules
Manufacturers Hanover Corp.	5.42%	1,900
Chemical Banking Corp.	6.66	1,058
BankAmerica Corp. .	6.91	1,301
First Interstate Bancorp	6.33	977
MCorp	4.87	646
Citicorp	7.72	561
Mellon Bank Corp.	6.34	511
Chase Manhattan Corp.	7.54	446
NCNB Corp.	6.76	358
First Fidelity Bancorp	7.22	228
Barnett Banks Inc.	7.27	174
Texas American Bankshares Inc.	5.55	125
Banks of Mid America	3.85	97
Bank of New England Corp.	7.76	69
National Community Bank	6.00	65
BayBanks Inc.	7.28	61
National Bancshares Corp of Texas	5.79	60
Cullen-Frost Bankers Inc.	6.63	45
BancOklahoma Corp.	6.14	45
Michigan National Corp.	7.54	40

Source: "The Impact of Risk-Based Capital on U.S. Banking: A Layman's Summary," *Keefe Bankreview*, Keefe, Bruyette & Woods, Inc., August 25,1988.

While the above discussion may seem to imply that regulation is the sole driving force behind securitization, it is not. Regulatory taxes, especially capital requirements, do have an important effect on asset securitization, and changes in regulation will significantly affect that activity. A bank's comparative advantage in originating and servicing loans, as well as the benefits from diversification and from establishing an additional funding source, however, are also important. Furthermore, the fact that nonregulated nonfinancial firms such as GMAC, Chrysler, and Sears securitize assets indicates that regulation cannot be the only reason to securitize assets.

Rules for Consolidation

Another recent development that will affect securitization is the change in the rules for consolidating majority-owned subsidiaries. The change in these accounting rules, which likely will be a boon to the asset-backed securities market, will probably affect nonbank issuers more than commercial banks that issue asset-backed securities.F See "A Bright Future for Securitization," *Asset Sales Report*, April 4, 1981.

As discussed in Chapter 7, an amendment to the generally accepted accounting principles for consolidation, which took effect in December 1988, states that the financial statements of all majority-owned subsidiaries of an organization must be consolidated with those of the parent unless control of the subsidiary is only temporary or does not rest with the owner. Prior to the change in the consolidation rules, the financial statements of finance, insurance, real estate, and leasing subsidiaries of manufacturers and retailers were not required to be consolidated with their parents' financial statements. Nonhomogeneous operations were excluded from their parents' statements because it was believed that their inclusion would distort them. Recently, however, views have changed. It is now believed that nonconsolidation of subsidiaries, even those whose operations differ substantially from their parents, would result in "omissions of large amounts of liabilities, especially those of finance subsidiaries," which would give shareholders and creditors an inaccurate picture of firms in which they have invested.[10]

This new accounting rule should increase the participation of finance subsidiaries of manufacturers and retailers, such as GMAC, Chryler Finance, Sears, Wards, and Penney, in the asset-backed securities markets. Many firms will not want their financial statements to look more like those of a finance com-

---

10 Financial Accounting Standards Board, *Statement of Financial Accounting Standards No. 94—Consolidation of All Majority-Owned Subsidiaries.*

pany than a manufacturer or a retailer.[11] Consequently, the securitization of assets, which results in a sale of assets by their originator, will become a more attractive way to fund a finance subsidiary's operations.

The Takeover Trend

In addition to changes in regulation and accounting rules, some trends in the economy will also significantly affect asset securitization. One such trend involves corporate takeovers.

Corporate takeovers, measured by the number of deals and the value of deals, have increased steadily from 1982 to 1986, and were at a seven-year low in 1987, at least in part because of the stock market crash that year and the huge increase in tax-induced acquisitions completed a year earlier. In 1988, however, takeovers are expected to exceed 1987 levels, but probably not those of 1986.[12]

Increases in corporate takeovers could translate into increases in securitization in several ways. First, securitization could be used to finance a company's operations after it has been involved in a takeover. "Highly-leveraged financings associated with corporate takeovers. . . usually result in sharp downgrading of a company's credit rating."[13] A corporation whose credit rating has been downgraded may be able to issue asset-backed securities that carry a higher rating than the company itself if the assets sold were of higher credit quality and/or if credit enhancement boosted the rating. Also, corporations can sell assets, such as trade receivables, as asset-backed securities and use the proceeds to pay down debt incurred in a corporate takeover.

A second way that increases in corporate takeovers could translate into increased issuance of asset-backed securitization is by increasing the dollar amount of loans that finance

11 "A Bright Future For Securitization."
12 "A Quick Rebound for M&A," *Mergers & Acquisitions*, (May/June 1988).
13 "A Bright Future for Securitization."

takeovers and that can be securitized—namely, LBO (leveraged buyout) loans and ESOP (employee stock ownership plan) loans. LBOs account for between 7 and 8 percent of all mergers and acquisitions and about 22 percent of the value of all mergers and acquisitions.[14] LBO loans, as discussed in Chapter 6, are often sold as participations, but were first securitized in October 1988.

ESOP loans have also been securitized. ESOPs can borrow money and invest the proceeds in the stock of the companies that establish them. As the ESOP sells stock to employees, the loan is repaid. Corporate takeovers that have involved management buyouts, such as the purchase of Avis by Wesray Capital and the purchase of Hospital Corporation of America by Health Trust, have used this form of financing.[15] As discussed in Chapter 6, ESOP loans have been securitized by several banks that are big lenders to ESOPs. If some big management buyouts use this form of financing, securitization of ESOP loans could expand greatly.

A third way that corporate takeovers could increase securitization of assets is the corporations' use of securitization as "shark repellent." A firm could sell assets via securitization and use the proceeds to buy back some of its stock.

Product and Geographic Expansion

The commercial banking industry has not been immune to the takeover movement. Throughout the 1980s, commercial banking firms have been expanding along product and geographic lines, often through mergers and acquisitions.

While commercial banking organizations engage in a wide array of nonbank activities, there are a few restricted activities that some banking firms believe are essential if they are to compete successfully as providers of financial services. One such

---

14 *Mergers & Acquisitions*, various issues.

15 "Banks Securitizing Loans for Employee Stock Plans," *Asset Sales Report*, September 8, 1987.

activity is providing investment banking services. Commercial banks have chipped away at many of the legal and regulatory barriers that separate commercial and investment banking. Through a series of regulatory rulings and court decisions, they have won approval to engage in many previously restricted securities activities.[16] Federal Reserve Bank of Chicago (November/December 1988). Consequently, many in the financial services industry believe that the repeal or substantial modification of the Glass-Steagall Act is imminent.[17] If this occurs, some commercial banking firms will expand their securities activities, and some will do so through acquisitions.

More importantly, along geographic lines, the commercial banking industry is undergoing considerable intrastate and interstate consolidation. During 1987, the banking industry registered more mergers and acquisitions than any other industry group. During 1987, over 300 deals, valued at $12.5 billion, were completed.[18] There are well over 5,000 banking firms in the United States, and it is highly likely that the banking industry will undergo much more consolidation, especially as more states open their borders to bank holding companies.

Whether the acquisition be a bank or a securities firm, securitization can fund the venture. At two to three times book, the sale of $200 million in, say, automobile loans could finance the purchase of a banking firm with $1 billion to $2 billion in assets. Similarly, $200 million could easily finance the purchase of a regional investment banking firm.[19]

---

16 See Betsy Dale, "The Grass May Not be Greener: Commericial Banks and Investment Banking," *Economic Perspectives*,

17 See The Financial Services Industry in the Year 2000, Federal Reserve Bank of Chicago, 1988.

18 *Mergers & Acquisitions*, (May/June 1988).

19 The median regional firm had about $4 million in book equity at the beginning of 1987 according to the *Securities Industry Yearbook*, published by the Securities Industry Association. A regional firm ranked 25th to 50th had between $44 million and $20 million in equity capital.

Implications for the Financial Services Industry

Recent changes in regulations and in generally accepted accounting principles as well as trends in the economy and developments in the financial services industry, will likely result in the continued growth of securitization. The first few years of nonmortgage-related asset securitization have been quite impressive in terms of the dollar amount of assets securitized, the types of assets securitized, and the number of issuers. As all involved in the securitization process have begun to move along the learning curve, the development and issuance of asset-backed securities has become less expensive. As they continue to make progress, more issues of asset-backed securities will be brought to market, and more types of loans will regularly be securitized.

When the securitization of assets becomes as commonplace as accepting deposits, the financial services industry will have a look very different from that of today. It will be transformed into a system in which banks increasingly compete with nonbanks in allocating credit, especially if banks are limited in their ability to securitize assets, and banks will operate more like brokers and investment bankers, warehousing loans to be packaged and sold to investors.

Specialization and Fragmentation

If commercial banks can securitize the majority of their loan portfolios, securitization could transform the banking industry into one that is more fragmented and specialized than it is today. Consider the following scenarios.

Banks accept deposits and make loans. Individual banks, however, specialize in making certain types of loans. For instance, one bank might emphasize consumer loans while another specializes in commercial loans. Or the lines of specialization could be narrower: one bank specializes in auto loans, and another in loans to the shipping industry. Each bank packages and sells its loans as securities to other banks, other depository institutions, and the public. The only whole loans on a bank's balance sheet at a given time are loans that are in the securitization pipeline. Banks fund new loans with deposits and with the proceeds from the sale of asset-backed securities. Consequently, most of a bank's income is derived from servicing the loans it originates and from underwriting fees.

This scenario does not imply that banks would no longer act as intermediaries of maturity and default risks. Securitization allows for the diversification of default risk through the pooling of loans, and securitization also enables a financial intermediary to match long-term borrowers with long-term investors.

A second possible scenario is that banks specialize in either deposit gathering or lending.[20] One bank might have a comparative advantage in operating a retail distribution network and collecting deposits, while another bank has a comparative advantage in making and servicing loans. The first bank then would collect deposits and invest them in securities backed by the loans originated by the second bank.

A More Efficient Banking System

If banks do have comparative advantages along either product or functional lines, then securitization could provide for a more efficient banking system. If there are economies of scale in the functions of deposit taking and lending, or in lending categories, securitization would allow a bank to generate the volume necessary to realize those economies. Securitization would also allow banking services to be provided with less capital and could allow funds to flow more easily to their most productive uses. It would lead to lower interest rates, more uniform rates nationwide, and greater availability of funds for loans.

A more efficient banking industry will be necessary as securitization causes banks to compete increasingly with

---

20 James McCormick, "Transforming Banks."

manufacturers and retailers who finance their own customers' purchases. Currently, banks compete for consumer loans and commercial loans with the captive finance companies of large retailers and manufacturers such as Sears and General Motors. Securitization will allow many consumers who would have taken out a bank loan to purchase, say, a new household appliance from a small retailer to bypass the bank and finance their purchases directly through the retailer, who can package his customers' loans and securitize or sell the loans to someone who specializes in such a process.

Also, the more liberal treatment of asset sales with recourse under generally accepted accounting principles relative to regulatory accounting principles may "permit greater relative advantages to nonbank originators of credit in liquifying and diversifying portfolios, matching assets and liabilities, and achieving funding costs (at AAA rates) lower than those of most banks."[21]

Conclusions

Securitization has already begun to change the financial services industry. It has enhanced the flow of credit, changed the way firms manage their portfolios, and increased the number of firms that compete for commercial and retail customer financing. While it is unlikely that securitization will completely replace other methods of financing or other means of managing portfolios, it will become widespread. When this occurs, its impact on the financial services industry, and the banking industry in particular, will become more apparent.

---

21 "Growth of Securitization," *The Vanderwicken Report* (New Hope, Penn.; October 1985).

Index

Accounting of securitization
consolidation rules, 179, 223-224
Financial Accounting Standards
Board
Technical Bulletin No. 85-2
(TB85-2), 169-170, 179
Financial Accounting Standards
No. 77 (FAS77), 167-168, 170,
171, 175, 179
generally accepted accounting
principles (GAAP), 163-164,
167-171, 179-182
implication of, 165-166
main questions in, 164
and Regulation D, 175-178
regulatory accounting principles
(RAP), 163-164, 167, 171,
174-175, 179-182
sales versus borrowing transaction,
167
See also individual accounting
methods.
Accrual bond, 64
Actuarial method, automobile
loans, 82-84
Adjustable-rate mortgages (ARM),
common
features of, 50 (table 3-2)

Adjustable-rate mortgage (ARM)-
backed securities, 76
Affinity groups, credit cards, 132
Agricultural Credit Act of 1987, 154
AMAX, 156
American Airlines, 144-145
Amortization event, 124
Annual percentage rate (APR), 86
Arnold Tours, Inc. v. Camp, 198, 200
Asset-backed bonds, 7
overcollateralization, 7, 17
structure of, example, 39-40
types of, 7-8
Asset-backed securities
participants
credit enhancers, 29-32
credit rating agencies, 32-35
investment bankers, 25-29
issuers, 23-25
originators, 22
servicers, 22-23
trustees, 35-37
risk, decreasing, 17-20
types of
asset-backed bonds, 7
automobile loans, 11
credit card receivables, 11
commercial paper, 9-10